# SCHOLARS
# AND PRIESTS

# SCHOLARS AND PRIESTS

by
Irene M. Franck
and
David M. Brownstone

A Volume in the Work Throughout History
Series

Facts On File®
*New York · Oxford*

**Scholars and Priests**

**Library of Congress Cataloging-in-Publication Data**

Franck, Irene M.
    Scholars and priests / by Irene M. Franck and David M. Brownstone.
        p. cm. — (Work throughout history)
    Bibliography: p.
    Includes index.
    ISBN O-8160-1449-3
    1. Teachers—History—Juvenile literature. 2. Priests—History—Juvenile
literature. 3. Scholars—History—Juvenile literature.
    4. Educators—History—Juvenile literature.
    5. Occupations—History—Juvenile literature.
    I. Brownstone, David M. II. Title. III. Series.
LA21.F72 1988                                                87-36011
371.1—dc19                                                      CIP
                                                                AC

Printed in the United States of America

10 9 8 7 6 5 4 3 2 1

Composition by Facts On File

# Contents

Preface ................................................................. vii

Introduction ........................................................... v

Curators ............................................................... 1
Librarians ............................................................. 7
Monks and Nuns ..................................................... 17
Priests ................................................................. 34
Scholars ............................................................... 94
School Administrators ............................................. 108
Teachers .............................................................. 115

Suggestions for Further Reading .............................. 187

Index .................................................................. 193

Titles in the *Work Throughout History* series

*Artists and Artisans*
*Builders*
*Clothiers*
*Communicators*
*Financiers and Traders*
*Harvesters*
*Healers*
*Helpers and Aides*
*Leaders and Lawyers*
*Manufacturers and Miners*
*Performers and Players*
*Restaurateurs and Innkeepers*
*Scholars and Priests*
*Scientists and Technologists*
*Warriors and Adventurers*

# Preface

*Scholars and Priests* is a book in the multivolume series *Work Throughout History*. Work shapes the lives of all human beings; yet surprisingly little has been written about the history of the many fascinating and diverse types of occupations men and women pursue. The books in the *Work Throughout History* series explore humanity's most interesting, important, and influential occupations. They explain how and why these occupations came into being in the major cultures of the world, how they evolved over the centuries, especially with changing technology, and how society's view of each occupation has changed. Throughout we focus on what it was like to do a particular kind of work—for example, to be a farmer, glassblower, midwife, banker, building contractor, actor, astrologer, or weaver—in centuries past and right up to today.

Because many occupations have been closely related to one another, we have included at the end of each article references to other, overlapping occupations. In preparing this series, we have drawn on a wide range of general works on social, economic, and occupational history, including many on everyday life throughout history. We consulted far too many wide-ranging works to list them all here; but at the end of each volume is a list of suggestions for further reading, should readers want to learn more about any of the occupations included in the volume.

Many researchers and writers worked on the preparation of this series. For *Scholars and Priests*, the primary researcher-writer was David G. Merrill. Our thanks go to him for his fine work; to our expert typists, Shirley Fenn, Nancy Fishelberg, and Mary Racette; to our most helpful editors at Facts On File, first Kate Kelly and then James Warren, and their assistants Claire Johnston and later Barbara Levine; to our excellent developmental editor, Vicki Tyler; and to our publisher, Edward Knappman, who first suggested the *Work Throughout History* series and has given us gracious support during the long years of its preparation.

We also express our special appreciation to the many librarians whose help has been indispensable in completing this work, especially to the incomparable staff of the Chappaqua Library—director Mark Hasskarl and former director Doris Lowenfels; the reference staff, including Mary Platt, Paula Peyraud, Terry Cullen, Martha Alcott, Carolyn Jones, and formerly Helen Barolini, Karen Baker, and Linda Goldstein; Jane McKean, Caroline Chojnowski, and formerly Marcia Van Fleet, and the whole circulation staff—and the many other librarians who, through the Interlibrary Loan network, have provided us with the research tools so vital to our work.

Irene M. Franck
David M. Brownstone

# Introduction

Religion and education have been intertwined for most of human history. Tens of thousands of years ago, *priests* were the individuals who gathered, held, and passed on to others the collective knowledge and wisdom of their people—and, it was believed, communicated with or at least influenced the gods. When to make war, when to make peace, when to plant crops and when to harvest them, when and whom to marry, when to travel and when not, how and when to hunt what animals—these and hundreds of other questions were asked of the priests. Consulting their storehouse of knowledge, the priests would answer as best they could, as advisers to rulers and others in the community.

For thousands of years that "storehouse" existed only in the memories of the priests. Acting as *teachers*, they passed their knowledge on orally, and each new generation of priests had to memorize it. The difficulty of learning and remembering so much helped make the priesthood a selective calling from the earliest times in human history.

This changed somewhat with the invention of writing in the Near East around 3000 B.C. Writing allowed knowledge to be written down and preserved for later generations. Even so, large amounts of knowledge could be passed on only to relatively few people in a culture. It took so long to make copies of a written work that few books were available for students. Most teaching still consisted of having students memorize vast quantities of material. That would remain true for thousands of years.

In the ancient Near East, reading and writing were still very rare skills, and practically the only place to learn these skills was at a religious temple. Anyone who wanted to become literate first came to the temple to learn to be a priest. Many who did so stayed within the religious community and worked as priests all their lives. Many others went out in the world to use their reading and writing skills in other ways—for example, as *physicians, architects, bookkeepers*, or *scribes*. Priests, then, were at the center of ancient society. They were also the society's main teachers.

In Classical Greek and early Roman times (and in China as well) religion and education were separated somewhat. Teachers in these societies were not generally priests, nor did they necessarily hold or teach any particular religious belief. Priests in general had far lower status. Teachers, on the other hand, were highly regarded. This was, after all, the age of philosopher-teachers, such as Socrates and Plato. Many teachers, however, were to some extent under the control of the state, which sometimes had strong views about what should and should not be taught. Socrates lost his life because he taught ideas that the state did not approve.

During the late days of Greece and the early days of Rome, just before and after the birth of Christ, we find some of the first specialists in gathering and caring for records of the past and present. *Librarians* managed the great storehouses of knowledge, such as the great libraries at Alexandria, Egypt, and Pergamum, in Asia Minor. *Scholars* worked in these libraries, studying the written records, interpreting them, and writing new works based on them. *Curators* worked to preserve works of art and other interesting items for future generations.

But in the waning days of the Roman Empire and in the medieval period that followed, these specialties and teaching as well once again came under religion's roof. In the chaos of Europe's Middle Ages, learning was centered in quiet, secluded institutions called *monasteries*. Here *monks* and *nuns*, shut away from the rough-and-tumble world, devoted themselves to religion. In some Asian religions, they even rejected the written word. But in European Christianity, they embraced it. Medieval monks and nuns became teachers, librarians, curators, and scholars, in addition to performing their religious duties. And most people who wanted to learn how to read and write came to a monastery to do so.

In the later Middle Ages and on into the Renaissance, schools were established outside monasteries. Even so, they were often staffed by priests, monks, or nuns; and the courses were taught in Latin, the language of the Catholic Church. Only gradually were some schools established that did not focus primarily on religious matters and the classics of Latin and Greece. In these new schools, teachers taught more practical subjects, such as mathematics and geography. Perhaps more important, they taught these subjects in the language of the people, not in Latin or Greek. Many such schools were established by cities and towns. That was especially true after the Protestant Reformation of the 16th century. So began the long battle between church and state for control of the schools.

After the Reformation, most monasteries in Protestant countries were closed, though monks and nuns continued to exist in Catholic countries, and in many places outside Europe. Catholic priests continued to work in their elaborate hierarchy, which stretched up to the Pope. Like the parish priests, Protestant priests, now generally called *ministers* or *pastors*, lived and worked in close and direct association with their congregations. They continued to have great influence on the schools. In fact, for centuries more, most teachers—in schools of whatever religion—had religious training and were expected to give religious instruction.

Only in modern time have religion and education been at all separated. The division has been sharpest in the United States, where "separation of church and state" is written into the Constitution's Bill of Rights. Even in America, however, a battle is constantly being waged between those who would have school teachers be religious instructors, and those who would have teachers avoid religious questions altogether.

With the rise of public education in the Western World in the last two centuries, schools have become a fixture in towns of every size. And most schools have become large enough so that *school administrators*—whose history stretches back to the Middle Ages—have become specialists in the educational field.

In the seesaw of history, priests—whatever their official title—have rather less status than they once did, while teachers have rather more. In the centuries after the Renaissance and the invention of the printing press, and the explosion of knowledge that followed, librarians, scholars, and curators have come into their own. Never in history has there been such a flood of information. Thanks to modern teachers, many more people can read and appreciate the works of the past and the present. But they still often need the help of other specialists in this family to interpret these works wisely and meaningfully.

# Curators

Although professional museum work developed mostly in modern times, especially in the 19th and 20th centuries, the earliest museums date back to ancient Greece. The Greek museum was called a *mouseion*, or "temple of the Muses," who were the goddesses of the arts and sciences. The museum was primarily a library or collection of manuscripts and an advanced research institute.

One of the earliest museums—and the most famous in the ancient world—was that founded in Alexandria, Egypt, in the third century B.C. Among the largest museums before modern times, it provided employment for staffs of *scholars, philosophers, librarians, scribes,* and *administrators*. These staffers, though, were professionals from specialized fields of interest, rather than specialists in museums. The scribes who worked at the museum were not trained specifically as museum scribes, for example, and could just as well have applied their skills to careers in publishing or teaching.

Until modern times, most museums existed in the houses of nobles and wealthy merchants, in the palaces of emperors and kings, or in churches, monasteries, and temples. None of these places called for professional staffing of any significance. Many Renaissance princes and nobles had museums in their homes. They were not professional museum directors or curators, but many liked to surround themselves with so-called *cabinets* of works of art, precious metals and jewelry, and assorted natural and rare curios. This interest would later stimulate the development of the professions of *museum operator* and *curator*. These Renaissance museums were visited mainly by scholars, artists, and culturally concerned aristocrats, who could view the collections during prearranged tours and presentations. There was little to interest the general public, and few museum owners cared to share their "cabinets of rarities" or "closets of curios" beyond their elite associates and friends. Museums, therefore, tended to remain small and private for centuries.

The first public museum was the Ashmolean at Oxford University in England, which opened in 1683. Although it was public, prospective guests had to be approved for admission tickets. The selection process was diligent and lengthy, often delaying visits for months.

The professional staffing of museums grew out of the desire to classify objects and departmentalize operations, a process that began late in the 18th century. Before then, museums generally held a hodgepodge of articles with no particular classification or chronological order. An ancient weapons display might stand next to one of contemporary art. Another change that was occurring at the same time was the rapid development of archaeology and the unearthing of ancient relics. These added new dimensions to the study of history and to the growth and structure of museums.

*Early museums were often collections of curiosities, and "curators" were commonly street barkers. (By Henry Muhrman, from* Harper's Weekly, *February 26, 1881)*

From the late 18th century to the present day, museums have become increasingly used as educational institutions, especially in North America, where democracy and universal public schooling have created an unprecedented demand for better public education. As museums have become more sophisticated and popular, the demand for well-educated and professionally trained personnel to staff them has increased.

Museums remained private and exclusive well into the 19th century, however. The Hermitage art collection housed in the Winter Palace of Catherine the Great at St. Petersburg, Russia (today, Leningrad, Soviet Union) could be viewed only by visitors dressed in formal court attire. The famous court museum in Peking, China, was so massive and restricted that it was known as the Forbidden City. Now called the Palace Museum, it was not opened to the public until 1924. This state of affairs was a strong obstacle to the professional development of museum personnel, who were usually court appointees.

Museum work was first professionalized in North America. Individuals such as Charles Willson Peale, who established an art museum in his home in Philadelphia in the 1780's, began the tradition of making museums independent enterprises, even though they had to depend on financial support and gifts of endowment from privately wealthy people. Operators of museums had a difficult time keeping them afloat for many years, however.

By the early 19th century some rather large museums were being developed in New York City. Many of them featured sideshows to bring in paying customers. John Scudder, who opened the New American Museum in 1810, provided a brass band that played "Yankee Doodle" for visitors while they viewed minerals, coins, shells, and stuffed animals. Admission was 25 cents. By the time Scudder died in 1821 the museum had become such a profitable family business that it was able to hire a *curator* for $11 per week. The "program" that attracted so many visitors included mummies, magicians, minstrels, and ventriloquists. John Scudder, Jr., was eventually removed from his post as museum head for drunkenness. The museum was then sold to P.T. Barnum, who made it even more of a freak show than a house of science or art.

Museums were extremely popular in the United States, and by 1876 there were over 200 of them. By this time they were also becoming more sophisticated. The general population was better educated, and the growth of cities created a massive, concentrated market for all sorts of entertainment and educational shows.

Meanwhile, the modern age of science brought new ideas in mechanical science, a greater understanding of natural science, and better notions of historical periods and events. Museums built on all of these advances and more. They required highly qualified professional staffing to fulfill their new expectations, goals, and potentials. European cities were also developing larger and more sophisticated museums—London, Munich, Vienna, and Paris all had large, diverse, and updated collections in many fields.

The first significant step taken in the standardization of the museum professions was the establishment of the American Association of Museums in New York in 1906. Just over 70 prospective members attended its initial meeting. The association was to have a greater effect on the quality and training of museum personnel than any other organization in the world. Today, the association aids universities in developing training programs for future museum professionals—sometimes called *museologists*—and operates the only national placement service in the country. Its publication, *Museum News*, along with its invaluable directory, is the leading employment service and source of professional guidance in the field.

*Curators* are the most specialized of the museum professionals. They head specific departments and are

*Before the establishment of large permanent museums, curators often assembled temporary loan exhibitions like this one at the National Academy. (From photographs by Pach, from* Harper's Week-ly, *November 2, 1878)*

responsible for acquiring collections and presenting them in a generally educational and entertaining manner. Curators are specialists who usually contribute original research reports to the literature in their fields of concern. Educational qualifications for curators are high, as is their public esteem. Salaries tend to be modest, and some curator posts are strictly voluntary and honorary, sometimes purely advisory. Some large museums also have staff *conservators*, who work at keeping old relics and works of art from wearing away with time and exposure to the elements; *restorers*, who return partially ruined or soiled items to near their original states; *registrars*, who receive and account for all museum pieces; *preparators*, who ready them for exhibition; and *designers*, who build cases for their display. *Teachers*, *librarians*, and various types of *clerks* and administrators also work in museums. Many institutions maintain their own workshops, which employ *carpenters*, *painters*, and other skilled artisans.

For related occupations in this volume, *Scholars and Priests*, see the following:
    Librarians
    Scholars
    Teachers

For related occupations in other volumes of the series, see the following:
in *Artists and Artisans*:
    Painters
in *Builders*:
    Carpenters
in *Communicators*:
    Publishers and Booksellers
    Scribes
in *Helpers and Aides*:
    Undertakers
in *Performers and Players*:
    Actors

# Librarians

In the ancient world the position of *keeper of the books* was usually held by palace or temple *scribes*. They were generally appointed for life, and their positions were often hereditary, particularly that of the court *librarian*. Some wealthy individuals also owned private libraries, and they frequently hired scribes or appointed house slaves—who were often educated prisoners of war—to take care of their collections. This was especially typical in the days of the Roman Empire.

Librarians of the ancient world had little public contact, since collections were available only to a select readership. The greatest libraries were those at Alexandria, Egypt, and Pergamum, in Asia Minor. These attracted the finest *scholars* of the Western world—both men and women—to work as *editors* and *researchers*. Some very eminent scholars became librarians in these prestigious institutions. Zenodotus of Epheseus, a famous grammarian of the third century B.C., was one of the more renowned librarians at Alexandria. He was the first to begin organizing the vast collection of books. His successors included some of the most notable names in ancient scholarship: Eratosthenes, Aristophanes of Byzantium, and Callimachus of Cyrene.

Julius Caesar opened the first public libraries, started with a library on Rome's Aventine Hill in 39 B.C. Many others followed, and the Roman emperors eventually had to appoint an imperial *library administrator* to oversee them all. Each library had its own *procurator*, who was responsible for acquisitions and administrative chores. There were also scores of scribes—some of them women—who busied themselves making duplicate copies of both Greek and Latin volumes. Private libraries continued to be important, though, and many were as elaborate as the public ones.

In China, libraries were the properties of emperors. Large staffs of scholars and *copyists* worked in them to amass a substantial literature. Much of this literature was derived from Confucianism and its commentaries, but many libraries contained primarily Buddhist materials, often copies of writings brought across Asia from India by devout pilgrims.

In the later centuries of the Roman Empire's decline, the great libraries suffered grievously. Much of Alexandria's library was destroyed in civil strife in the third century A.D. Most of the remaining collection was destroyed as pagan in the fourth century when Christianity became the official religion of the Eastern Roman Empire, later called the Byzantine Empire. Libraries around the Mediterranean suffered a similar fate.

But some libraries survived, notably those of the Nestorian Christians, who fled east and south of the Byzantine Empire, after being branded as heretics. Their libraries laid the basis for the important survival of the library tradition under Islam. In the ninth century the

Moslem Abbasid caliphs began the systematic collection of Greek works, especially scientific and philosophical writings. Through the end of the 10th century, professional librarians were employed to acquire such works, many from the Byzantine Empire and from Cyprus. They also oversaw their translation and duplication by teams of scribes. The greatest of these Moslem libraries was in Baghdad, but libraries were also attached to private courts and to the many universities established under Islam. In later centuries, court and university libraries of Córdoba, in Islamic Spain, came to the fore. Just as Alexandria's collection had been destroyed centuries earlier so much of Córdoba's court library was burned in the late 10th century in a conservative reaction by some against learning. Córdoba's libraries were later revived and the works collected there provided an important base for Europe's intellectual Renaissance.

Christian monasteries and cathedrals housed the most noteworthy libraries of medieval Europe. Librarians were drafted from among the most scholarly *priests*, *nuns*, and *monks*, who were ardent copyists more than *catalogers*. Books were generally still kept in chests, rather than on shelves, where they were more prone to destruction and theft. So the monastic librarian was more often called an *armarius* (the Latin word for chest) than a *librarius*, although both terms were used. In any case, the librarian was responsible for taking care of the building as well as its collection, and also directed both the *scriptorium* (where manuscripts were copied by teams of scribes) and the book bindery. Frequently the librarian was also asked to act as *precentor*, or director of the singing of masses. Parish libraries were smaller collections that were more available in smaller communities and to a more general readership; the parish priest usually acted as the head librarian of these.

Noble families and eminent scholars continued to house significant libraries. They usually hired scribes or scholars to maintain and even duplicate their collections.

These were the only truly professional librarians of the time. But, because the monastic "custodians of the library" were a much larger and better organized group, their practices led more directly to the development of the librarian's profession.

Larger and more sophisticated libraries were commonplace in the early modern times, following the invention of printing in the 15th century. Libraries were still usually attached to church, court, or private estate. But by the 18th century—with the new intellectual interests in science and philosophy nurtured during the Age of Reason and the Enlightenment—they became more active and more important. Professional opportunities for librarians increased both in number and significance, and many leading scholars were appointed to librarianships.

Gottfried Wilhelm Leibniz was a renowned turn-of-the-18th-century philosopher, mathematician, and diplomat. But he earned his living, for the most part, as a court librarian in Paris; in Hanover, where he served the Duke of Brunswick; and at Wolfenbuttel in Germany, where he developed an alphabetical catalogue. One of his successors at Wolfenbuttel was the eminent Fritz Ebert, whose early 19th-century book on *The Training of the Librarian* was one of the first of its kind. The book bitterly denounced the sad state of the profession and lamented that libraries often treated books as buried treasures, largely unavailable to the public and almost impossible for the scholar to sift through for lack of organization and standardization. Ebert insisted that the librarian should be a full-time trained professional, but he was ahead of his time in holding these views.

Despite Ebert's criticisms, German libraries were the most advanced of their time, and the profession of librarian was better developed and systematized in 19th-century Germany than anywhere else in the world. "The chief librarian," said Robert von Mohl, professor at Tubingen, in 1836, "whatever else he may be, must think and plan night and day for his library; in its behalf he must buy and exchange, beg and—one might almost add—steal." Germans rightly boasted that among the ranks of their professional librarians were many highly regarded figures, such as the great writer Johann Wolfgang von Goethe, who served as head librarian at Weimar and the University of Jena at various times.

Many of the notable librarians in modern European courts were men of leisure and aristocratic background who undertook the "profession" because of its social esteem and their love for books and knowledge. Gabriel Naude, librarian for Cardinal Mazarin in Paris, spent years traveling to England, Flanders, Germany, and Italy to acquire some 40,000 volumes. Sir Thomas Bodley provides a similar example from Elizabethan England. A dedicated librarian of substantial means, he vowed "to set up my staff at the library door" at Oxford University,

*Early librarians often worked in the private libraries of rich and powerful individuals. (Author's archives)*

where he had studied and taught. The Oxford library was in a state of total disrepair when Bodley unselfishly offered five years of his time, energy, and fortune in helping to get its doors opened again.

Librarians in Colonial America were originally employed by colleges and universities. They were often junior faculty members who were given the additional chore of keeping libraries open for an allotted period of time each week. These institutions often considered their libraries to be relatively unimportant. In 1765, for example, Harvard University required its librarian to keep specified hours and maintain a heated reading room only on Wednesdays. Faculty members alone had access to the university library until the late Colonial period, and extremely tight restrictions were placed on the circulation of books. Students may not have minded too much, however, since almost every book in the collection was theological. Librarians here were even more truly part-time house-sitters than professional guides or researchers of any sort.

By the time of the Civil War, college libraries were still small, open to students only a few hours daily at best, and generally restricted to theological and standard reference works. The librarian was still an assigned faculty member, whose duties were more of a nuisance than an occupation. There were also student libraries on most campuses. They were usually run by student volunteers and were frequently better and more useful, containing more contemporary volumes than the main library. It was not until the end of the 19th century that professionals staffed university libraries. Indiana University was one of the forerunners of this development, hiring its first professional librarian in 1880 and adding three additional staff members eight years later. By 1900 most university libraries were open to extensive student use and were professionally staffed.

Nonacademic libraries were becoming increasingly important in the 19th century, as industrial and urban societies created new demands for both special and general information. Public libraries were just beginning to emerge, particularly in America, where democratic idealism spurred an acceleration and widening of education. British parish libraries and American subscription libraries, such as the Boston Athenaeum, set the stage for the rapid development of the public library movement.

In 1850 the Public Libraries Act was passed in Britain, and by the end of the century there were 300 public libraries in that country. The first public library in America was established in 1833 in Peterborough, New Hampshire. The first professional librarians of the Boston Public Library (established in 1852)—Charles Jewett and Justin Winsor—lent considerable prestige and direction to the profession, which was rising in response to the mushrooming growth of public libraries. In the early 1900's, Andrew Carnegie granted over $50,000,000 for the development of community public libraries throughout the nation. Similar movements were under way in Europe and in Russia as well, although they did not really have widespread success until after World War I. University and college libraries were also becoming larger and better organized. With an increasing number of students, higher educational institutions had a greater demand for libraries and for the services of professional librarians.

As late as the 19th century, however, librarians were still unprepared for the professional duties that were becoming more and more essential. Ebert had written in his essay *On Public Libraries* that such places consisted of "dusty, desolate, and unfrequented rooms in which the librarian must spend a few hours weekly to discharge his duties—so that during this time he can be alone!" But times were changing, and so was the nature of librarianship. Libraries were becoming educational resource rooms rather than mere museums of manuscripts.

Libraries were also becoming highly systematized and sophisticated. Professional librarians had to be trained in acquisitions and in new, highly technical classification systems. Foremost of these was the famous Dewey decimal system, used to catalog and organize books for easy access. Most important, librarians had to re-evaluate their occupation in light of their new roles as community educators. Melvil Dewey himself best summarized the revolution in the profession:

> The time was when a library was very like a museum, and a librarian was a mouser in musty books, and visitors looked with curious eyes at ancient tomes and manuscripts. The time *is* when a library is a school, and the librarian is in the highest sense a teacher, and the visitor is a reader among the books as a workman among his tools. Will any man deny to the high calling of such a librarianship the title of profession?

The first available professional training in librarianship was offered at the University of Gottingen in 1886 by the famous German scholar and librarian Karl Dziatzko. In the following year Dewey established the first library school in the United States. The chief difference in European and American styles of training in the field was—and still is—that the former is more general and scholarly, while the latter is more specialized and technical. Germany has been a leader in attracting people of high scholarly achievement into the profession. Hitler encouraged the development of a highly trained librarianship because he thought it represented a significant channel in the political control of the masses. Britain's first professional training was offered in 1919 by the London University School for Librarianship. Most other European countries are still in the relatively early stages of this movement.

Public librarianship has been more generally emphasized in America than in Europe. On the other hand, American research librarians have been criticized for being too preoccupied with the techniques of storing and locating information and having too little scholarly comprehension of, or interest in, the materials at hand. In this sense, the American librarian tends to be more like the medieval caretaker of collections than the contemporary educator and researcher. Russian librarians have been trained to adopt the best of both the American and European systems and professional standards.

The 20th century has seen an ever increasing refinement and specialization of the profession. There are now subject specialists and in-residence researchers, as well as *reference librarians*, who assist the now-common general reader in using the library properly—in locating materials and conducting meaningful research.

The American Library Association recognizes the following classifications of librarians: *clerks, technical assistants, library associates, professional librarians* (who hold at least a Master's degree in library science), and scholarly subject specialists. Libraries have administrators, circulation clerks, reference guides, and shelvers. But the profession is still a relatively new one, and all of these specialists are very recently derived.

Professional library associations have developed all over the world in modern times and have proven to be effective instruments of standardization and cooperation. Most of them publish journals updating the latest trends in the profession. Although there is still some in-service training of librarians, most of them must receive university education with graduate work to at least the master's level. These librarians—in the 20th century many of them women—receive comfortable salaries, enjoy rather high prestige, and earn the sense of satisfaction that comes from directly helping other people.

For related occupations in this volume, *Scholars and Priests*, see the following:
Curators
Monks and Nuns
Priests
Scholars
Teachers

For related occupations in other volumes of the series, see the following:

in *Artists and Artisans*:

    Bookbinders

in *Communicators*:

    Authors

    Clerks

    Editors

    Printers

    Publishers and Booksellers

    Scribes

in *Helpers and Aides*:

    Servants and Other Domestic Laborers

# Monks and Nuns

Monks and nuns have occupations purely dedicated to God or some form of enlightenment or spiritual salvation. Their professions are based partly on vows to forgo personal material rewards. Whatever earnings or gifts they are offered become part of the community or monastic treasury, surrendered to the maintenance of the pious community and its reverent sanctuaries.

Monasticism dates back to at least the sixth century B.C. in India, when Siddhartha Gautama (known as *The Buddha*) first instituted the *Buddhist Order*, or the *Sangha*. This was a retreat for those who wished to seek enlightenment and truth with the support of a cloistered (that is, secluded from the outside world) brotherhood. Only after considerable pleading from one of his disciples did Gautama reluctantly agree to ordain women as *nuns* (*theri*). The *monks* were derived from a small class of wandering ascetics—people living a contemplative life and denying themselves earthly pleasures. They were known in ancient India as *samana*. They joined Gautama in the Sangha during the three months of the year (July through September) that the monsoon rains made wandering and begging from door to door virtually impossible. It was during these annual gatherings that a regular community life evolved.

The Sangha was a unique institution in that it offered membership to all believers, regardless of their caste. This was revolutionary in a society where only Brahmins, the highest caste, had customarily been permitted to seek careers in religion. For some time, Gautama alone reserved the authority to admit initiates into the order, but this was soon delegated to other head monks. One might enter the order at basically two levels: as a novice (*samanera*) or as a monk (*bhikku*), the first being essentially a stepping stone to the second. All monks had shaven heads, wore yellow robes, and carried begging bowls; these characteristics distinguished them from common beggars and tramps. They took special oaths (such as that of celibacy) and followed the Middle Way of the Buddha, as outlined in the Ten Precepts. These forbade killing; stealing; unchastity; untruthfulness; drinking alcoholic beverages; overeating (or eating at all past noon); joining in dance, drama, or song; adorning oneself with perfume or jewelry; sleeping on high or broad beds; and owning personal property or money.

From the earliest times, regular householders were permitted to hold lay-member status while living and working in the secular world. These part-time monks had only to live by the first five of the ten precepts, and to attend regular meditation sessions. Some became novices for only short terms, such as during a funeral or a time of personal trial. Their inclusion in the Sangha was extremely significant because most were nobles and gentry (*Kshatriya*), who heaped great gifts from the world into the central treasury of the order. This, in a sense, financed the operation and the building of temples and sanctuaries.

The Sangha grew great in its first two centuries, through both its ordained and lay membership. In time, though, it was split into different schools and sects over differences of opinion as to the degree of strictness and asceticism that monks ought to live by. The Theravadin and Mahayana emerged before the Christian era as the two major traditions in the history of Buddhism.

The older *Theravadin* orders taught a fairly active approach toward seeking salvation. Theravadin monks attempted to overcome egotistical feelings of selfhood in order to become unified into the one solitary Truth or Being. They woke up before sunrise, performed an exhausting routine of chores, and spent the rest of the early morning hours in solitary meditation before candles and Buddha-images. After brief group breakfasts and chants, they departed into the villages to beg for food. Wherever they went, they kept their gaze to the ground, not wanting to be distracted from their serious missions by the gay and pleasing sights of the world. After returning to the monastery, the monks joined their brothers in the last meal of the day (around 11 A.M.), and then retired, each to his tiny cell. There they spent the afternoon in studying and copying religious texts, and in meditating upon prescribed themes: the Love of all creatures, Pity for those in want, Joy for the prosperity and good fortune of others, the Impurity of the secular world, and the Serenity obtained in true knowledge of Being. Evening hours might be spent in consulting with superior monks and in further meditation before sleep.

Theravadin monks were deeply committed to educating the lay people and to maintaining personal purity. They confessed their sins publicly, during regular gatherings of the brotherhoods. Like all Buddhist monks, they went to the greatest extremes to avoid harming any form of life. They watched their steps to avoid stepping on crawling insects, for example, and strained their drinking water to save any bugs that might have found their way into it.

While these general rules pertained to monks of non-Theravadin sects, too, some subtle and some profound differences existed—mostly at the philosophical rather than practical level. The *Mahayana* monks were more concerned with compassion for living beings rather than with their own personal salvation. Most monks sought Buddha-hood as the form of perfection and ultimate passage into Nirvana (the One Truth or the One Being). However, many of the Mahayana preferred the state of being a Bodhisattva—that is, one who elects to postpone his entrance into Nirvana so that he may help to enlighten and save those in this world. Therefore, their roles as educators and leaders of state were more pronounced. They also opened their sanctuaries to public worship for the great masses of people.

Buddhism spread far over Asia, especially to the north and east of India. Buddhist monks commanded great respect in ancient and medieval Asian life. Some also wielded considerable political authority. Among these were the *theri* (nuns) of the fourth and fifth centuries A.D. imperial courts of China, an odd circumstance since nuns—then and now—have had little place in the Buddhist orders. In fact, various Buddhist texts state that only males may become Buddhas.

The greatest significance of the Buddhist monks was in their scholastic achievements, their education of those in all social classes, and their delivery of a personal and emotionally involving religion for the masses. The general population of India otherwise could only turn to the formal, elitist, and somewhat sterile rituals of the Brahmin caste of the Hindus. In essence, the Buddhist monks helped to hold together the vast reaches of various Eastern empires, and to unify their peoples for a time into a similar culture.

## Christianity

Monks and nuns did not perform the same central functions under Christianity. After Catholicism became the official religion of the Roman Empire in the fourth century A.D., the hierarchy of *priests*, *bishops*, *cardinals*, and *Pope* held the main reins of power. Still, Christian monks and nuns had a profound influence on the growth and direction of the church and its regular priesthood, particularly in the Middle Ages.

Christian monasteries and nunneries, under the spirited direction of *abbots*, *abbesses*, *priors*, and *prioresses*, were havens of Western civilization during the tumultuous medieval era. They served as centers of learning and culture as well as economic activity at a time when—outside of cloistered walls—there seemed to be little beyond petty warfare and primitive farming. They copied texts (both secular and sacred), experimented with industry and technology, and fostered education at all levels. In so doing, the medieval monks are credited by many observers with saving Christendom and Europe from total barbarism, and possibly from ultimate absorption into Islam. But the occupation of monks and nuns was—first and foremost—religious.

Some monastic orders existed in the Mediterranean world before they became common among Christians. One such was the first century A.D. order of the Therapeutae, founded by Egyptian Jews near Alexandria. By the end of the third century A.D., some orders of Christian monks had begun to break away from main church activity. Some early *ascetics* and *hermits* were not really monks, but idiosyncratic individuals. Consider Simeon the Stylite, who lived atop pillars and had his food lifted to him by attendants; or the more ordinary hermits who lived in tiny cells, trees, or caves, in which there was barely room to move. Monks soon began to seek more community organization to avoid the insanity and strange extremes experienced by many of the early pioneer hermits. The monasteries offered monks companionship and direction, rules and regulations. In return, the monks did the work of the cloister, begged for its food, received gifts for its treasury, and carried out its social programs for the homeless and the poor. The early Christian monks had to obey certain ethical rules of conduct and were usually forbidden to read anything other than sacred writings.

Many monastic orders, however, became quite lax in upholding strict moral behavior and in fostering an intense imitation of Christ. Over the centuries this would inspire various reform movements. In the sixth century A.D., the order of St. Benedict set guidelines and a proper example for the reform of all Christian monasticism. The so-called *Benedictine Rule* included many suggestions that were to have a lasting impact on the occupation. More than that, its overall tenor was one of close supervision and severity, as witnessed by the rule that "monks should always be occupied, either in manual labor or in holy reading." Furthermore:

> One or two of the older monks shall be appointed to go about through the monastery during the hours set apart for reading, to see that none of the monks are idling away the time. . . . And if any brother is negligent or lazy, refusing or being unable to read or meditate at the time, let him be made to work, so that he shall at any rate not be idle.

Perhaps the most important feature of the Benedictine order was their emphasis on reading and learning, and their inclination to foster a scholarly and intellectual haven for the monks.

Medieval Christian monks usually came from the aristocracy. If they were unable to gain a suitable post in state or military service, many young men turned to monastic life, either for itself or as a means of obtaining appropriate civil appointments. Women entered nunneries, and elite families often chose to send young girls there to receive moral training—and sometimes to meet some promising and eligible young men from nearby monasteries. Both monks and nuns had respectable enough occupations. But there was also scandal within the cloisters—overdone by contemporary writers perhaps, but also indicating the laxity in the profession. Although monks and nuns took vows of celibacy, sexual activity and clandestine marriages between monks and nuns themselves were not unheard of. Reform movements were constantly in the air, as different orders sought to restore the purity and purpose of the monastic life.

A more widespread problem than outright lewdness and licentiousness among monks and nuns was a general preoccupation with worldly concerns. After all, through gifts, heredity, and even bribes, the monasteries, abbeys, and nunneries were some of the largest property holders in the world. These properties were used for manufacturing, milling, mining, and agriculture. The monks were leaders in such economic activities, so they necessarily became enmeshed in the political and economic structure of society. Abbots and priors, as well as abbesses and prioresses, became not only spiritual directors but also *business managers* in every sense of the word. Also, many abbeys were inherited by nobles, who directed them solely as business ventures. Still, among the worldliness and economics of the propertied cloisters, the repentant, solitary, and contemplative life of the monk was maintained, revived, and reformed to some degree in many orders.

*Dominican* monks, called *friars*, were supposed to live lives of poverty and begging, but many attained great repute and sometimes wealth through holding secular positions, particularly as university *instructors* in the church-oriented halls of learning. The distinguished theologians St. Thomas Aquinas and Meister Eckhart were Dominicans, but so, too, were the hateful and heartless "dogs of the Lord." These were the papal *inquisitors*, who mercilessly attacked heretics—people who

*The original caption noted that monks were once hermits and forest dwellers but are now not particularly spiritual. (By Jost Amman, from* The Book of Trades, *late 16th century)*

questioned the established view of religious questions—in Spain and elsewhere. Some Dominicans were at the forefront of the attack on *scientists* and *mathematicians* who stepped forward with what seemed to be unholy explanations of the universe. These critics thought that such learning was to be deduced from Biblical authority and the church dogma only. Dependence on logic and reason was, to them, close to heresy. (Not all Catholics—or even all Dominicans—agreed, of course.)

The Dominican orders were governed by a *master-general*, who, in turn, supervised a string of *provincial-priors* and *provincial-prioresses*. They were the actual directors of daily routine at the monasteries and nunneries. Priors and prioresses were rather democratically elected to their posts by their brothers and sisters, and held four-year terms of office.

The *Franciscans* were a unique and important group in that after their first order of monks and second order of nuns, they established a third order of lay people. They admitted all people (and even animals) to their prayer services. Following their beloved founder, St. Francis of Assisi, they preached freely to criminals, lepers, outcasts of all sorts, and even beasts of the field. Their mission was compassion, and like St. Francis, they vowed to be always "married to Lady Poverty." A *minister-general* was their superior administrator, while *provincial-ministers* acted as directors of operations.

The *Jesuits*, although not monks, were a militant brotherhood who fought against evil as "soldiers of the cross." Their founder, Ignatius Loyola, was their *first general*, and the "spiritual exercises" that he prescribed with detailed descriptions were done under the guidance of spiritual *drill-masters*. They not only supported the papacy during the Protestant Reformation, but became great missionaries of the church, carrying its influence eastward as far as Japan, and westward to the Americas as far as California during the 16th and 17th centuries. Their persecution of the French Huguenots (Protestants), however, earned them a rather sour reputation in the 18th-century Age of Enlightenment and religious toleration. They were eventually forced out of several European countries, including the great Catholic strongholds of France, Spain, and Portugal. Jesuits were always held in high distinction for their learning and educational activities, and only the brightest could enter the prestigious order. Once a Jesuit had gone through his basic training, he was placed in the occupation best suiting his talents, as judged by his immediate superiors.

Some other monastic reforms had been instituted earlier by the *Order of Cluny*, whose monks were bound to restore the almost forgotten Benedictine Rule. They had tremendous support from the medieval aristocrats and landed lords, and themselves became great patrons of the visual arts and other cultural undertakings. The

*Cistercians* were even more somber. They vowed utter silence and followed extremely restricted diets, so that they might not be seduced into ways of the world or bodily satisfaction. None of these reform movements had total or lasting success. Many monks and nuns still had rather worldly preoccupations or ulterior motives in entering the cloistered life.

Even so, there always remained in the cloisters a core of true "professionals," monks and nuns who spent their lives in prayer and contemplation, in studying and reading, and in sharing loving care and companionship with lay people in the villages and with brothers and sisters in the holy community. Their guidance came primarily from Christ and the saints, and their lives were dedicated to the love and imitation of those sources. Quietly and compassionately, without regard to their personal health, wealth, or well-being, they prayed, preached, and taught, always mindful of their holy mission in life.

## Islam

Islam, which had emerged during the Middle Ages, borrowed directly and heavily from the monastic models of Christianity. Syrian mystics wandered throughout the deserts in the seventh century A.D., reciting Allah's "beautiful name," while giving no heed to physical or worldly cares. They sought no shelter, food, or medical care, did no work, and did not complain about the physical or verbal abuse heaped upon them by hecklers.

Mesopotamian (Iraqi) mystics continued the tradition into the following century when the first of the *Sufis* appeared. The Sufis were a mystical group seeking divine communication or revelation. They differed from the earlier Moslem mystics in that they chose to organize themselves into settled communities for companionship and group efforts such as farming and preaching. The very name *Sufis* means *wool-bearers*—those who suffered the wearing of itchy, coarse woolen robes to divert their attention from the pleasures of the world. Still, they were highly criticized at first by the orthodox Moslems (the *Sunnis*), who attributed this scolding of Islamic monks to Mohammed, the Prophet: "Either you propose to be a Christian monk; in that case, join them openly! Or you belong to our people; then you must follow our custom. Our custom is married life!"

Regardless, the Sufi movement grew, and rules of celibacy—although also Christian in origin—were common. The reason for its great success was that it filled two voids in Islamic life. First, the Sufi monks prepared and administered regular religious services and rituals to the common lay people. This was important in a religion that had little ceremony, no priesthood, and little community outreach. Second, the Sufis stressed the emotional aspects of a faith that hitherto had been so enmeshed in law and politics that it had scant popular appeal. The Sufis' love of music and dance as stimulants to immediate mystical experiences was a welcome variation on the mundane proceedings of the Islamic courts. For these reasons, Sufism not only survived, but it has even been credited with much of the broad appeal that Islam itself gained, by giving it a popular base, and a sort of quasi-priesthood to act as examples of the religious life.

The Sufis were generally self-denying and vowed to poverty, as most monks in all faiths are. Small but colorful groups of them gained much attention, notably the so-called ecstatic ones. They practiced self-mutilation and total world renunciation, in attempts to be rid of their selves and be fully absorbed into Allah.

Many Islamic orders made quite a spectacle of their divine ecstasies. The *Whirling Dervishes* used wild music while they danced in ritual frenzies. The *Howling Dervishes* tortured and whipped themselves into similar states. The *dervishes* were monks who wandered and begged, while being organized into fraternities under the spiritual guidance of a shamanistic master (like a medicine man) or guide. They had a large number of orders during the Middle Ages. The dervishes entertained onlookers with such feats as swallowing

*Islamic dervishes often used singing and dancing to induce ecstacies or hypnotic religious trances. (From* Men: A Pictorial Archive from Nineteenth Century Sources, *by Jim Hartner, Dover, 1980)*

snakes and passing knives through their flesh. Many of their orders admitted lay members who lived and worked in the world but took part in their ceremonies. Despite all the interest in the ecstasies of dervishes, most Islamic monks lived quiet lives of solitary prayer, field work, and intellectual and literary pursuits.

## Medieval Buddhism

Buddhist monasticism gained considerable variety in the Middle Ages, particularly in China, Japan, and Tibet. The *Jodo-Shin* monks had no regard for personal salvation but dwelled only on their faith. They were allowed to marry and live and work in the world—that is, outside of the monastery. Their hereditary lines of abbots in some periods had great political and military authority.

The *Ch'an* (as they were called in China) or *Zen* (as they were called in Japan) followed a passive inward journey to salvation. They sought only silence and submission as a way to enlightenment, rather than actively seeking enlightenment in other ways. They dwelled on the nondualism of the Buddha-reality—the oneness and sameness of "I" and "not-I." Zen monks were not supposed to read or write but only to speak with their spiritual masters and *gurus*. Those who offered philosophical—that is, rational—arguments and questions were rebuked with nonsense answers, since the order felt that no truth could come through language. Those who insisted on rational explanations rather than silent enlightenment might be beaten into submission until they began to understand. Zen monks would spend up to 18 hours a day in silent meditation—in the so-called *zazen* way to truth—for several days in succession. They meditated in pairs, facing but not "seeing" each other, breaking only for brief intervals to consult with their guides.

An intellectual order of monks called the *Tendai* had great influence at court in Japan. Their religious center at Mt. Hiei was the center of Japanese culture and education for centuries, with some 30,000 monks in regular attendance. Many Tendai monks left the order after extensive educational training and became *priests*, *educators*, and *government leaders*. Several other orders (including the Zen) were offshoots of the Tendai order. The Japanese *Shingon* were soldiers and civil servants who believed that the Buddha manifests himself in material success; most of these monks were sons of nobles and courtiers. The *Nichiren*, in contrast, believed that the world was evil and so, too, were forces that attempted to disrupt order. They arose in the 13th century as champions of the emperor, who was on the verge of being overthrown by rebellious nobles. Nichiren monks, thereafter, had great political and military power and even in the 20th century sponsored a regular political party.

The *Tibetan* monks, a colorful group, adopted yoga—a series of exercises to discipline mind and body—and tantric (mystical-magical) practices as ways of enlightenment. Many Tibetan monks and *lamas* (head monks) were common householders, living and working in the world while seeking spiritual direction in the monastery. *Superior-lamas* (abbots) were commonly chosen as infants. Certain monks were designated to seek infants who possessed divine qualities and to declare them reincarnated former head-lamas, thereby granting them the authority of that office. The Dalai Lama is the most famous example of this unusual selection process.

## Modern Times

In the West, the Protestant Reformation, which began in the 16th century, led to a considerably reduced status for monks and nuns. In Protestant countries they were persecuted as representatives of Roman Catholicism, and in Catholic countries they were criticized for abusing their calling by taking on worldly professions and pretensions. (Buddhist monks were undergoing similar ridicule at the time, notably the many Bodhisattvas who were lining their pockets with the sale of "Prayers for the Dead.") The Christian professions of monks and nuns underwent severe setbacks in the modern era, and by the 18th century became a relatively minor presence in society, with only a small core of members.

Yet the advent of rationalism and materialism in modern Western civilization, though it ushered in an age of religious apathy, also brought a time of unprecedented religious toleration. Quietly, the monasteries began to regain members, as they updated their approach to the religious life and corrected old abuses. In the 17th century, the Cistercians underwent a revival movement that is felt today most keenly through the *Trappist* orders established throughout the world. The Franciscans have three thriving orders today: the strict *Capuchins*, the moderate *Friars Minor*, and the relatively lenient *Conventuals*, who are even allowed to own property. The Church of England and the French Evangelical Church have also revived monastic orders in the last century and a half.

The monastic professions have remained significant in Eastern culture and have regained status and respect in the West. Monks and nuns tend to live quiet and cloistered lives of prayer, meditation, and self-sufficiency. It has become more popular in recent years for monasteries to offer their premises and guidance to visiting groups or individual soul-searchers for short-term retreats. The profession tends to be intellectually rigorous. Even those monks and nuns who have traditionally shunned the written word are often intellectually gifted. Even today, many a prominent Tibetan logician and scholar is an illiterate monk who has fashioned a remarkable art of oral expression.

Most monasteries are still closely tied to the efforts and proceedings of churches and temples. Many of those in the East are regularly visited by throngs of pilgrims. Tibetan monks are well known for their gay and colorful ceremonies and rites, during which thousands of pilgrims join them in holy chants and pageants. While Western monks usually have little political, social, or economic influence on their communities, those in the East frequently do. The 14th Dalai Lama is the political and spiritual ruler of Tibet, although he and his court have spent years in exile in India. Tibet still has over 200 head lamas, with varying degrees of community leadership, supervising 500,000 monks, although the whole country has a population of only 3,000,000 people. Some monks hold hereditary posts, some are elected. The Nichiren monks in Japan entertain thousands of chanting pilgrims every day at their temple (the largest in the world) at the foot of Mt. Fuji. They also have a strong political party, run monk-candidates for office, and still have a powerful impact on Japanese sociopolitical life.

Monks today may be leaders of state, as Buddhists frequently are; spiritual guides to lay people and initiates (those in the early stages of becoming monks); simple farmers who have no ties to the world except for the selling of some of their produce and baked foods (Trappist bread is a very popular item in many marketplaces); or severe ascetics and self-mutilators in the old mystical tradition, a tiny minority today. More than ever, all are beleaguered by the age-old dilemma of whether to try to improve this world or concentrate on passing solemnly into the next. There are as many resolutions to this problem as there are orders of monks, with some trying to have absolutely nothing to do with earthly matters and others trying to save the world from all evil. Whatever the path taken, monks and nuns are a unique faction of humanity whose occupation is generally unfamiliar in the modern world of material and rational thought—but is an important part of life in many underdeveloped parts of the world.

For related occupations in this volume, *Scholars and Priests*, see the following:
Curators
Librarians
Priests
Scholars
Teachers

For related occupations in other volumes of the series, see the following:
in *Artists and Artisans*:
Calligraphers
in *Builders*:
Architects and Contractors
Masons
in *Communicators*:
Authors
Clerks
Editors
Scribes
in *Financiers and Traders*:
Accountants and Bookkeepers
Bankers and Financiers
Merchants and Shopkeepers

in *Harvesters*:
  Farmers
  Gardeners and Landscape Designers
in *Healers* (forthcoming):
  Nurses
  Pharmacists
  Physicians and Surgeons
in *Helpers and Aides*:
  Social Workers
in *Leaders and Lawyers*:
  Political Leaders
in *Manufacturers and Miners* (forthcoming):
  Factory Workers
  Miners and Quarriers
in *Restaurateurs and Innkeepers* (forthcoming):
  Bakers and Millers
  Distillers
  Winemakers
in *Scientists and Technologists*:
  Astrologers
  Astronomers
  Biologists
  Chemists
  Engineers
  Geographers
  Mathematicians
  Physicists

# Priests

The priesthood is an ancient profession of great cultural, political, and economic—as well as religious—significance. Cave art from tens of thousands of years ago strongly suggests that a special class of *magicians* existed who tried to win the favor of gods or spirits during tribal hunts. Using a simple form of sympathetic magic, these people would paint beasts being stalked by brave hunters. Presumably these paintings aimed both to please and impress the gods, and so persuade them to translate such pictures into reality during the course of the actual hunt. These magicians seem to have used similar approaches to win favor with the gods in healing, childbearing, war, and other matters of importance to the clan. Priests around the world followed this pattern into modern times, acting as intermediaries between their local congregation and the gods or spirits of the culture.

Some religious professionals took a different course: *monks* and *nuns* chose to separate themselves from society, generally attempting to foster individual and wholly personal relationships with their objects of worship. The most dominant members of the priesthood began to develop institutional hierarchies, organizations that have had a profound effect on the development of human culture throughout history.

Some of the earliest and historically the most influential religious institutions were those of the ancient Near East. The Egyptian and Mesopotamian priests formed a powerful class, which vied continually with the nobles for supreme social, political, and economic status. In both of these cultures, *polytheism*—belief in the existence of many different gods—was strong and rarely challenged. These gods were seen as supernatural entities, which had created and now controlled the universe as well as human events. They were not perfect, however, and had no set design for the evolution of personal or community histories, so people felt the gods were open to pleas, persuasion, arguments, even pressure.

The people who attempted to influence the gods were the magicians and *exorcists*, who drove away evil spirits. Others specialized in understanding, rather than challenging, the will of the gods. These were the *astrologers*, *diviners*, and *augurs*. Still others specialized in the administration and maintenance of the temple complex, along with its many varied economic activities. These specialties were not mutually exclusive, and all who did these jobs were priests of one order or another. As such, they all had common duties, responsibilities, and training, which united them as a distinct social class and professional group.

## The Near East

In Egypt, the pharaoh was not only the high priest, but was even thought to be a deity. In the early dynasties, the pharaoh was referred to as the Son of Ra, god of the sun. According to this so-called Royal Doctrine, the pharaoh was supposedly an incarnation of Horus, an earlier form of the sun god. Clearly then, there was little separation between church and state. Priests had enormous political influence, just as civil rulers had enormous religious influence, since they were considered gods themselves.

Many priests were *scribes*, charged with the recording and interpretation of the sacred "word." This function had enormous importance since according to Egyptian mythology, Thoth—the scribe of the gods—was the creator of the universe. The scribal duties of the priest were essential to the functioning of the temples, which were large and thriving commercial and cultural centers. Some priestly scribes were charged with keeping records of moneys due to the temple for agricultural products, for flour from the temple grist-mill, or for hand-crafted goods. Others were in charge of purchasing supplies for temple employees to work with and provisions for its staff, while still others took charge of the orders and the storage and shipping of goods received.

Besides the countless administrative functions of scribal priests, involving record keeping, business transactions, and treasury deposits, the temple carried on more scholarly enterprises as well. Those priests so inclined worked as *teachers* in temple schools and universities and as *librarians*, *archive directors*, and *curators* in the temple.

The temple was clearly the greatest seat of learning and scholarly activity in ancient Egypt. Its army of priest-scribes formed at least as grand an administrative force as that retained at court. But priests undertook many other activities as well. Many worked in the fields, almost as hard as the *slaves* did; others were *shepherds* in the hills, and *beekeepers*, *bakers*, and *vintners* within the temple complex.

One especially important priestly specialty was medicine. Priests were credited with keen understanding of divine will and fate, and were presumed to have magical and sacred powers to intervene in the course of events on behalf of individuals as well as causes. So it was quite fitting that priests be appointed to the care of the sick, even in cases where their actual medical knowledge was limited. In fact, there developed a rather skilled corps of priestly *physician-surgeons*, who had as much insight into the natural causes and cures of diseases and illness as anyone at the time.

Another major occupation in the Egyptian temple was the *mortuary priests*. The Egyptians firmly believed in an afterlife. They invested a great deal of time and energy in preparing for it, as well as in caring for those who had already passed into it. The mortuary priests were stationed in the *necropolis*, the pyramid-city where the dead were buried. For endless hours they sat in prayer for the souls of deceased nobles, whose families had the means to hire them for such purposes on a contract basis. They exhorted the gods to care for their clients' safe journey through the underworld, while also seeking the assistance of the dead souls in the moral concerns of their

*The vestiture of a high priest was a solemn and grand occasion in Egypt. (From* History of Egypt, *by Clara Erskine Clement, 1901)*

families still on Earth. When the family had the money to order such services, these priests also performed the daily *Mortuary Rite*. During this ceremony they removed the approved family image of the deceased or frequently even the actual mummy from its tomb, and ritualistically fed, dressed, and adorned it, while offering a steady stream of prayers and incense. Before returning the image or mummy to its proper place, the priest performed the *Opening of the Mouth* rite. In this rite, the mummy's lips were touched with a sacred instrument that, Egyptians believed, permitted it to breathe in the vitality of the gods and to continue its existence as a living soul.

Buried away in the dark tombs of the pyramid-city, the mortuary priests lived a dismal existence, almost like the dead that they cared for. Probably the most exciting part of their occupation was in taking their proper turn as *guard* of the tomb. Since the dead were treated like the living, they were given many lavish worldly possessions, such as tools, weaponry, jewelry, and precious metals and ornaments. Massive wealth accumulated in the tombs, and many a sacrilegious *thief* lurked about, seeking to bypass the armed priests.

Closely related to their services for the dead, the mortuary priests were also engaged in the practice of *necromancy*—maintaining communications with the deceased for the purpose of divination and fortune-telling. They sought to reach dead souls through *Letters to the Dead*, which they wrote on parchment or vessels used in mortuary offerings.

Another closely related activity was composition of the *Book of the Dead*, or, as the Egyptians called it, the *Chapters of Coming Forth by Day*. These texts were elaborate spiritual exercises and directions designed to guide souls through their after-death travels. They included hymns, prayers, and spells, along with sometimes beautiful illustrations and funerary and divine judgment scenes. Among these was the popular judgment of Osiris, god of the dead, in which the weighing of the heart was the central theme. Some of the greatest ancient literature is embodied in the compiled texts of the *Book of the Dead*. Mortuary priests were often paid extremely well for their efforts on these texts, since they were thought to have a great impact on the nature and comfort of one's immortal existence. Naturally, the most profitable contracts for such work came from the rich—the nobles, aristocrats, and pharaohs themselves, so these priests tended to work for the elite social classes rather than the lower classes.

The ultimate task of the priests was the care of the gods themselves. The daily Mortuary Rite performed for the deceased was actually a mock performance of the *Rite of the House of the Morning* being performed at the same time at the palace. In that ceremony, the pharaoh—acting as the supreme priest—led a procession to the tomb of the deity being cared for. The officiating head priest was the one who actually performed the rite. Accompanied by assistants, dancing *priestesses*, and *singers*, he broke the clay that sealed the deity's tomb and then tended to the divine statue in the same way that the mortuary priest cared for a mummy. Having dressed, adorned, and fed the god—who was actually supposed to reside in the statue, just as a person's soul was thought to reside in the mummy—the priests offered prayers. The officiating priest, having fulfilled his mission, retreated from the divine tomb by walking backwards. He then resealed it with clay so that nobody could enter again until the next day, when the rite was performed anew. The tomb was guarded by teams of priests in rotating shifts around the clock, while other priests offered 24-hour prayers and liturgies.

Considering the vast importance of death and the ministering to the "needs" of the deceased, it is not surprising that the Egyptians had a well-developed class of mummification priests. These were often priests who also practiced as temple *physicians*, since it took considerable knowledge of the human body to practice the art of mummification as well as the Egyptians did. Sometimes priests might be occupied for months properly treating a corpse—especially one of a noble or royal person.

The priesthood of Mesopotamia (the region of modern Iraq) was less involved in death rituals and funerary processes and paid no attention to the deceased. The Babylonians, for instance, believed that the here and now was all that existed, and that death was only a void and final end. The Babylonian priesthood, then, concerned itself with supplications and sacrifices to the gods aimed not at immortality but at success and prosperity in this world.

The Babylonian priests—the most literate class in that society—also busied themselves with the recording of divine messages, stories, and omens. These sacred writings were of two types: those that the priests claimed related the exact words (the *shruti*) of the gods, precisely as the priest had heard them, and those which the priest paraphrased (the *smriti*) in his writings, being able to recall only the general sense of the divine utterances. While the *shruti* established the priesthood as a truly holy and authoritative class, the *smriti*, which was most in need of interpretation and comment, demanded the intellectual investment of the more scholarly priests. In Babylonia and elsewhere in Mesopotamia, the priesthood became a source of both sacred authority and intellectual insight. As in Egypt, its members became leading *educators, administrators, scholars,* and *librarians.*

Religion in ancient Egypt and Mesopotamia pervaded every aspect of cultural, economic, and political life, not just the moral side of it. If anything, morality was more a civil matter, handled by the state's *rulers* and *lawyers*, than a religious concern. The famous "eye for an eye, tooth for a tooth" decree was part of King Hammurabi's landmark law code, not a piece of sacred writ. If there was any separation between church and state, it was in terms of morality. The gods seemed unconcerned with the issue of right or wrong; as portrayed in the mythologies of the Near East, they were totally pragmatic and opportunistic. The priesthood, then, was not necessarily concerned with the moral behavior of the temple worshippers but with the fulfillment of their duties to the gods, which they performed to win favor and blessings while averting divine wrath and vengeance. Civil rulers were concerned more with morality as a means of holding together increasingly complex and cosmopolitan societies.

Priests in ancient times focused primarily on the behavior of the gods, only secondarily on that of mortals—and even then chiefly as it affected divine action. As a result, among the most important functions of all ancient priests were divination and magic. The Egyptians believed that gods, no matter how troublesome, were open to persuasion. Even Seth, the god of droughts and storms, who so often wreaked havoc with economic life along the mighty Nile River, was dutifully worshipped in order to keep him in check.

Priests, then, practiced magic, astrology, and divination to learn what the gods intended for the future, and how they might be pacified or perhaps controlled. At times, Egyptian priests might try to intimidate the gods or even punish them by withholding offerings of food, riches, or sacrifices—or occasionally even by whipping the divine idols or statues. More typically, though, Egyptian priests, acting as diviners and astrologers, played a relatively passive role—trying, for example, to determine whether or not it was a favorable time to go to war, or if there was a conspiracy brewing against the pharaoh, or if it was a good time for planting a crop, and so forth. Of course, they also tried to gain the help of the gods in such matters as winning victory in war or reaping a bountiful harvest. In those cases they were properly humble and reverent.

The Mesopotamian priesthood was much more active in its use of magic and divination than the Egyptians were. In fact, Christian authorities would later equate many orthodox features of Mesopotamian worship with witchcraft and sorcery. Yet, the magical devices used were designed only to be pleasing or persuasive to the objects of worship. Nudity, for example, was a primary symbol of purity and reverent unification with the supernatural powers. As in Egypt, morality apparently had little or no place in worship, divination, or ritual; anything that might win the favor of the gods was given a try. Still, many early Mesopotamian religious practices seemed horrid to the Egyptians and even more so to the Hebrews.

Sumerian priests always performed their holy duties in the nude—some say in imitation of the gods who were so perceived. In fact, physical beauty was of extreme importance in the priesthood, since the priests themselves were supposed to be living symbols of divinity—much as modern athletes are supposed to be examples of physical perfection. People with any physical defects or deformities were banned from initiation into the profession. On Crete, priestesses officiated at formal ceremonies naked from the waist up, a practice that was very common in the practice of witchcraft for many centuries, and was thought to be especially effective when priestesses were casting magic spells.

Many Mesopotamian priestesses were counted among the temple *prostitutes*, especially those of the fertility cult of the goddess Ishtar. Their role as prostitutes was somewhat ritualistic and symbolic, being related to the appeal for increased fertility.

The Mesopotamians were much more concerned with evil than the Egyptians were. They supposed evil spirits to be everywhere—in rocks, trees, and certain persons. The gods could protect them from evil, but so could the established priesthood, whether through its own initiative or by effectively invoking the aid of the gods. Temple magicians and exorcists were available to cast spells, drive out evil spirits, and even change the course of nature. They were usually paid quite well for their services, and often went through notable dramatics to display their talents. Babylonian priests sometimes held vigils on the roof atop the house of a person afflicted with illness or disease. They remained there for hours chanting, praying, and burning sacred torches to draw the evil out of the stricken soul and return his body to normal health.

Perhaps the strongest organization of Mesopotamian priests were the *diviners*. They kept extensive records of their interpretations of such omens as how oil drops dispersed in water and the forms taken by a sacrificial sheep's liver. These and other omens supposedly foretold the future and were consulted carefully by kings, governors, and military leaders before they made pivotal decisions on important matters. Whole orders of the Babylonian priesthood specialized in the interpretation of dreams, while others concentrated on the significance of natural events such as lightning or drought. Those adept at interpreting astrological charts were especially revered.

The priesthoods of rival cults commonly developed complex cosmogonies (theories about the origin of the universe) to illustrate that their patron deity was superior to another one and to get or retain political influence. This is clearly seen in Egypt, for example. The followers of Thoth were in the two cities called Hermopolis, while Ra worshipers were in Heliopolis, and the Ptah cult in Memphis. The priests at Memphis had the early support and patronage of the pharaoh and developed into a sort of highly distinguished intelligentsia. The priesthood of Ra, however, developed the royal doctrine of the divine origin of the pharaoh. As a result it became the dominant religion and subsequently one of the greatest political forces in the kingdom. The same priesthood proved equally cunning in holding its acquired position of influence when confronted with strong competition from the rising popularity of Amon worship at Thebes. It simply changed the name of its patron deity to Amon-Ra, and successfully combined ideas from the two religions in a way that not only permitted it to remain the leading priesthood, but even increased its power by bringing in a whole new following of Amon worshipers.

At one point, a pharaoh named Akhenaton tried to enforce a monotheism on Egypt, by declaring Aton to be the one and only true god of the empire. The first true religious reformer in history, Akhenaton was well ahead of his time. The powerful priesthood of Amon was instrumental in the ultimate overthrow of his revolutionary ideas. His successor, Tutankhamen, returned to the Amon priesthood all of its former privileges, powers, and glory. Egypt was destined to remain a kingdom of competing priesthoods until the Christian era. In fact, at one time, no fewer than 2,000 different gods and goddesses were being worshiped in the land, although a handful of priesthoods continued to monopolize the power of their professions.

Egyptian priests held rank according to their appointment by the pharaoh, although a system of seniority apparently figured in promotions to more responsible, prestigious, and lucrative positions within the professional hierarchy. Sometimes their appointments were hereditary, particularly in the case of those who cared for the temple gods said to reside in cult statues. These *servants of the god* were also high-ranking officials and advisors of the pharaoh. The high priest of an important state god also had considerable political importance. Like the mortuary priest, he had to obtain a high degree of purity through ritual, behavior, and circumcision. Priestesses had their own separate hierarchy, which included temple *singers* and *dancers*. Priests presiding over important festivals and ceremonies, such as the Mortuary Rite, were ranked (in declining order of importance) as the *Father of the God*, the *Slave of the God*, the *Ordinary Priest*, and the *Lector-Priest*. Officiating at the festivals was also one of the great honors in the profession.

In Mesopotamia, too, there was a distinct hierarchy in the profession. Rulers of state were the official high priests, while each cult had its own *urigallu*, the grand guardian of the temple complex. Like the temple high priests, these were responsible for the administration of the entire workings of the temple complex, as well as for arranging community festivals. They were also the *personnel officers* for all the other orders of priests under them: the exorcists, diviners, astrologers, scribes, artisans, physicians, and so forth. The priestesses, again, had their own separate hierarchy. Some of them were of royal lineage and attained extremely high ranking and officiating responsibilities, while others were mainly singers, dancers, and prostitutes.

The life of the ancient Near Eastern priest was a highly prestigious and sheltered one. Priests were paid salaries from the temple treasury and were provided with living quarters, food, and clothing. They could also earn some rather substantial side money, gifts, and even offices in the form of private offerings—all this in a world where luxury, or even comfort, was hard to come by. The Egyptian mortuary priests and Babylonian *sorcerers* were especially likely to gain great wealth through these means. Most priests married, and a good many handed their offices down to their sons. Most priests had to fulfill some rather mundane obligations, like tilling the fields and tending to the granaries, during at least part of their careers. In all, though, the profession was stimulating, financially rewarding, secure, and prestigious. Many an aristocrat was pleased to have his son train for entrance into the priesthood.

## Greece and Rome

During the Greek and Roman eras, the nature of the profession altered considerably. The Greeks, polytheists like the Egyptians and Mesopotamians, couched their mythologies in anthropomorphic images—that is, they perceived their gods as humanlike. The Greek gods were a divine family, with all its squabbling, temperamental, sometimes loving, but occasionally vengeful members. It is little wonder that there was no real love of the great gods, and that personal and household deities became much more endearing to the Greeks. Prayers and offerings were much more likely to be directed toward a minor god such as Zeus Ktesios—guardian of family possessions—than one of the state gods such as Apollo, who seemed to care little about an average person's concerns.

State religion lost much of its appeal during the Classical Age of Greece. This was partly due to the skeptical ideas of the *sophists* and *philosophers*, who had such a great impact on the intellectual and cultural life of the Greeks. It was also partly due to the unresponsive attitude of the priesthood itself. Eventually, the profession hardly existed at all, except for the *temple managers* appointed by the state to maintain the sanctuary and its grounds. State priests also officiated over the Olympic Games, Athenian festivals, and other ceremonies in which the gods were honored with displays of athletics, magic, poetry, music, art, and drama. But as these declined, and other religious festivals became increasingly competitive, commercial, and secular, the priesthood lost much of the prestige it once had held in presiding over them.

A revival of the profession was kindled somewhat by the rising popularity of the *mystery cults*, including the Eleusinian, Dionysiac, and Orphic mysteries. These proposed to introduce worshipers into a more personal relationship with the deities through the performance of secret rituals led by an elite group of priests. These cults tended toward extreme degrees of frenzy induced by immediate religious experiences. Only initiates were allowed to learn of these secret rituals, and they were not permitted to relate them to outsiders. To this day, little is known of what actually took place during these secret sessions.

The only truly organized Greek priesthood was that of the sanctuary of Delphi, a cult center of Apollo, which became widely known for its oracle. The oracle was delivered to inquirers by a prophet or priest, who received and interpreted responses from a priestess known as the Pythia. She supposedly received divine messages and answers to questions while in a state of extreme ecstasy and frenzy, purportedly brought on by Apollo's divine magic, but probably resulting from the influence of a hallucinogenic drug.

The Romans added considerable pomp and glitter but little real substance to institutional religion or the priesthood. State temples were magnificent and laden with precious jewels, gold, silver, and some of the finest art work in the world. The temples were, in actuality, a state treasury. War booty and gold bullion were stored there, and many nobles placed valuables and moneys there for safekeeping. Many temples also included art galleries and museums, which were opened for public enjoyment at certain times. Little actual worship occurred within temple walls, however. In all of Rome—a city of over a million inhabitants—there were only about 100 such sanctuaries. The priests acted chiefly as guardians and administrators of the state's wealth and holdings.

The most important of the Roman priests were the *augures*, the official diviners of Rome. They consulted and interpreted the oracles credited to the Cumaean Sibyl and collected in the *Sibylline Books*. These Greek

*At the School of the Vestal Virgins, novices learned how to carry out their religious duties. (From* Museum of Antiquity, *by L.W. Yaggy and T.L. Haines, 1882)*

oracles were stored in Rome's Capitoline temple and kept under the care of a special group of priests. In times of emergency, these augures even called forth the gods in a *lectisternium*, during which the gods were thought to sit at a symposium with the priests to discuss possible courses of action. Other augures interpreted the divine meaning of such things as a chicken's eating habits and the flight of birds. The *haruspices* constituted a special group of augures who interpreted omens exclusively through the study of the livers of sacrificed animals.

The priesthood brought in significant revenues to the state. Sacred festivals were large commercial enterprises, and diviners substantially bolstered temple treasuries with their magic and fortune-telling. The priests focused on no moral or philosophical creed, only the good of the state.

Augustus Caesar initiated the practice of mandatory emperor worship. Caligula and Domitian pushed the doctrine to its extreme and demanded that they be treated like gods even throughout their mortal lives. Religion became ever more a political tool, and priests followed the orders of the court. State-authorized augures alone could practice divination, and only when requested by a civil *magistrate*. Violators were arrested and prosecuted. At one point, state officials were even empowered to guarantee certain individuals eternal salvation through orders of a priest—for a fee, of course.

On the whole, the Roman priests were a highly esteemed and elite group of professionals who were grandly rewarded for their labors. Even the *attendants*—priests who admitted guests into the temple, where they might pray for hours on end to gain some favor from a divine statue—gained considerable wealth. They received not only monies for granting the privilege of admission but many expensive gifts afterward if the temple visit proved to have successful results.

Despite their accumulated fortunes or honorable occupations in the Roman civil service, most priests were less than inspiring to the worshippers. They were generally known as devout agnostics—that is, people who claim to have no knowledge of God or the gods. This stimulated little religious fervor or response from the community. Partly because of this, an illegal but enthusiastic priesthood of certain Eastern religious cults began to displace the state religion in the hearts of many people. These new priests were extremists in many ways, and their cults were frequently outlawed. The cult of Bacchus, best known for its wild orgies, was at one time suppressed by the state, as were the activities of its priesthood. Roman religion would continue to be characterized by a mixture of apathy and fanaticism for centuries, until a new religion from the East—Christianity—later drew together the many diverse peoples in the empire of the Romans.

## India

While the Roman Empire remained in a state of religious anarchy, Asia was home for the development of the major religions of the world. *Hinduism,* centered in the area that would later become India, was the most widespread organized religion for many centuries. Its priesthood was highly regimented and stratified. The reading and interpretation of the Hindu sacred writings called the *Vedas* was the priests' most important responsibility. Accordingly, they were obliged to perform the rites spelled out in that body of writings.

During the sacred ceremonies, at least three gods were present: Soma offered immortality through the imbibing of a special holy drink, which could be prepared only by priests; Agni was the god of the holy fires and the chief mediator between the gods and their worshippers; and Brahmanaspati was the embodiment of the sacred word, the power of which could be activated only in his presence. Since his presence could be invoked solely by the priestly caste, the priests' role in human communication with the gods was absolutely indispensable. Because of their spe-

cial relationship with the "divine priest" Brahmanaspati, Hindu priests were referred to collectively as the *Brahmin* caste by the end of the seventh century B.C.

The Brahmins were pitted against the *Kshatriyas* (nobles) for several centuries in a struggle to gain social and economic supremacy. As the settlements of the Ganges River Valley began to unite into a vast and impressive Indian empire, however, the Brahmin caste became increasingly important to the Kshatriyas. The powerful unifying influence of Hinduism had allowed the creation of a great territorial kingdom, and it had become apparent that only the Brahmins could hold it together. The Brahmins came to possess such great power and influence because of their claim to have an exclusive correspondence with—and even power over—the gods.

The Brahmins alone were versed in the complex art of Hindu sacrifice rituals, some of which took months to complete. It was believed that their power of prayer and of delivering sacred utterances was so great that they could literally alter events. Their powers, in short, were thought to go beyond those of merely persuading or pleading with the gods. The Brahmins practiced techniques—elaborately described in the sacred *Brahmanas*—that have been best described as magical coercion. Gods as well as humans, it was believed, were forced to obey the Brahmins' demands if prayers, the attending rituals, and sacrifices were all performed properly. Their ceremonies, therefore, were no mere motions, nor were they simple celebrations. They were the very core of Indian life and the backbone of the state.

The Brahmins were an extremely elite caste, and ordination into the priesthood followed a rigorous path of study. Most of the *Vedas* were not written down until the third century B.C.; before that they had to be committed to memory—a practice continued as a matter of tradition for some time following. As if this were not enough, prospective priests had to understand and expound in oral tests with superiors fine points of philosophy underlying the sacred writ; to recall perfectly the minute details of lengthy rituals; and to note accurately the different roles of various families within the Brahmin caste. Although the priesthood—like all other stations of life in Hindu society—was strictly hereditary, those wishing to actively enter the profession had to earn their ordination. Once they attained such a high status, though, they would have the authority to consecrate kings as well as to perform domestic rites.

Hindu rituals were highly organized and elaborate, and employed the efforts of many specialists within the priesthood. In a typical sacrificial rite, for example, a high priest would officiate on sacred grounds outside of the temple. Altars were erected there for the burning of sacred fires and the holy sacrifice; seating was provided for the invisible, attending them. The priests made many offerings to the gods, including melted cheese, wild grain, soma libations (these sometimes took months to prepare, the process itself being part of the total ceremony), and sacrificial animals. Priests sang and chanted prayers for hours on end as they performed their ceremonial duties. Finally, the offerings were removed from the sacred fires and administered to the attending body of worshippers who had waited for many hours—sometimes several days—to share the immortal and intoxicating soma with the priests and visiting gods.

The Brahmins gained enormous prestige and wealth through the administration of rites, the ultimate one being the *Asvamedha*, in which over 600 horses were sacrificed in the consecration of the monarch. The ceremony lasted over a year and cost the reverent ruler dearly. He could hardly help but invest in such a service, however, as the Brahmins dutifully advised him: "This atonement is for everything. He who performs the Asvamedha redeems all sin."

Nonetheless, as the Christian era approached, the authority of the Brahmin caste began to wane. The sacred priests had always defended their exclusive roles and divine authority on the grounds that they were rightfully inherited according to the sacred Hindu Law of Karma. Their argument, (which took for granted the theory of reincarnation) was that, since people were reborn into certain social stations or castes according to the accomplishments or works (*Karma*) of their previous lives, those born into the Brahmin caste had obviously earned their privileged status. It was only fitting and moral, therefore, that they be properly rewarded for their holiness by both men and gods. Any attempts to alter this divinely ordained social order constituted a dire sacrilege.

A new tradition was arising the in East, however—one that was strongly supported by the Kshatriyas (nobles). This was the belief that, although the Brahmin caste had made substantial progress in understanding and communicating with the deities, yet another approach—perhaps an even more profound one—could be taken. This was the way of the *ascetics*, who found the truth through an inner spiritual journey which included personal meditation, prayer, and sacrifice, without any involvement or mediation of a priestly authority. In other words, the religious experience was interpreted as an inner and personal one, rather than a ritualistic manipulation of the outer world by an official body of priests. The sacred Upanishads—the last of the *Vedas*—seemed to concur with this view. Even the title—*Upanishads* translated as "sitting next to" or "session"—indicated that enlightenment was something of a learning process, in which one might best be tutored by enlightened ones. Ritual and ceremony were clearly secondary in this scenario, and the role of the priest would either be modified or altogether undermined.

From about 500 B.C. to about 500 A.D., *Jainism* and, more important, *Buddhism* rivaled the Hindu notion of the religious life, not only in India but in much of Southeast Asia. The priesthood hardly even existed in these ascetic forms of spirituality, being replaced by orders of *bhikkhus*, or *monks*. Gautama, the founder of Buddhism, organized a community of followers into a *Sangha* (religious brotherhood). Since his teachings gave little heed to the role of the priestly functions, he and his followers were considered heretics by the Brahmins. In fact, Buddhism did not have a priesthood but rather a series of Sanghas, which were founded by their respective *buddhas*—spiritual leaders, or *gurus*. The idea was that truth was a matter of kindling inner fires and making personal sacrifices rather than kindling altar fires and making animal or cereal sacrifices. The buddha—the one who had discovered this extremely difficult path to enlightenment—was obligated to show others the way through his teachings and through his establishment of a Sangha. *Bhikkhus, pabbajakas*, and *samanas* were various kinds of wandering ascetics who left their homes, earthly possessions, and pleasures to live in poverty, selflessness, and world denial. The Hindus often spoke of the "Samanas and Brahmans" when referring to the two vastly different types of religious leadership. Buddhism, then, became a monastic rather than an institutional religion; its story is less of priests than of *monks* and *nuns* (discussed in a separate article.)

## Eastern and Central Asia

Many types of religious leadership in the East stressed a simpler, more direct, and more highly emotional approach to enlightenment than the Brahmin caste had presented. In China, diviners and magicians called *Wu* formed the most ancient priesthood. These *shamans*, or *"medicine-men,"* tried to exert control over the spirits that were thought to exist in every conceivable nook and cranny—in the lakes, behind trees, or even in a person's hair. As mediators between the human world and the spirit world, shamans would dress in costumes rich with symbols as they prepared to enter a trance or other magical posture. Their ability to foretell and mediate the actions of the spirits often made them the most suitable physicians available to care for the ills of body as well as of fortunes. They were thought to have the power of reversing the aging process and performing other miracles over mind, body, and soul. The Polynesian shaman was a wise man and healer, but also a sorcerer (*tahutahu*), who was highly accomplished in the arts of black magic and curses. The shaman, then, applied his special skills and position not only for good deeds but sometimes for evil ones as well.

While the ancient Chinese shamans were believed to possess extraordinary powers over the spirit world, a special order of shaman-priests were ordained to officiate at public ceremonies and rites. The ordination of all shamans was both controlled and limited in growth by the state from a very early period. All shamans were supposed to be state licensed and registered and were largely patronized by court society. *Confucianism*—the closest thing to a state religion in China—had no real priesthood at all, so that the profession had little real or politically independent growth in ancient China.

Among the Medes of ancient Iran (related to the Aryans of India), the Magi were a tribe that monopolized the priesthood and in particular the administration of the sacred and magical beverage *haoma*. This hereditary caste included some eight separate special priestly

*This turn-of-the-century Chinese priest from Shanghai looks little changed from his counterparts of centuries before. (From* The New America and the Far East, *by G. Waldo Browne, 1901)*

"arts," most of which were related to the gathering, preparing, pressing, testing, and blessing of the haoma. The *athravan* (fire priest) officiated at another important ritual cult—that of fire.

When Zoroaster initiated his new religion in Iran (in the seventh or sixth century B.C.), he was met with fierce opposition from the established Magi and a local cult of greedy and unscrupulous magic priests—the Karpans. Zoroaster preached an emotional and personal religion based on the ever-present dualism of good and evil. The most distinctive feature of his teachings was *mono-theism*—the belief that there was but one god. Though once a shaman, Zoroaster came to regard himself as simply a *zaotar*, or priest. His challenge to his followers was that they light the fire of truth in their souls rather than on the altar, and that they do this through their own personal attempts to attain knowledge of the one true God, not through the magic or ceremonies of a mediating priesthood.

Despite its disdain for the cult priests, Zoroastrianism itself evolved a priesthood, which became quite militant and intolerant in its attempts to enforce a belief in the "true" religion. The Magi were eventually won over and became the established priesthood of the zealous religion. Zoroastrianism dominated Iranian culture until it was displaced in the seventh century A.D. by the Islamic faith. Meanwhile, both the Hebrew and Christian religions and priesthoods were being greatly influenced by Zoroastrianism.

## The Jews

The priesthood of the Jews was largely hereditary. The Old Testament relates how Yahweh (God) commissioned Moses to ordain Aaron and his sons "to minister in the priests' office" (Exodus 28:1). This created a conflict in the profession since, before the Jews' exile in Egypt, the militant Levites had constituted the chief priestly caste in the community. (The name *Hebrew* came from the word *Apiru*, by which the Jews—and other refugees—were known in Egypt.) The Levites were relegated, after the exile, to the status of temple servants. The Aaronic priests, meanwhile, were obliged to follow closely the "Priestly Code," which gave precise and detailed directions related to the priesthood. It indicated exactly what priests should do in performing their duties, what sort of dress they were to wear during certain ceremonies or while ministering in the temple, how they were to purify themselves, what constituted their proper and moral behavior, and what professional privileges they were entitled to.

The priesthood became exceedingly powerful as Israel developed. The high priest became the leader not only of the temple but of the state as well. The Jewish historian Josephus justified the *theocratic* rule of Israel in this way:

Could there be a finer or juster polity than one that sets God as governor over all things, assigning to the priests generally the administration of the most important affairs, and entrusting to the high priest the leadership of the priests.

In fact, the Hebrew priests endeavored to control every facet of life in the community. Like the priests of Zoroastrianism, they believed that there was only one true God, and his divine will constituted an absolute moral law. Also like the Zoroastrians, they were convinced that this good moral law was constantly being undetermined by evil forces, and by false priests and prophets, who were bound by those forces. As a result, the Hebrew priests were constantly on the lookout for moral weaknesses among both clergy and lay people. If they detected any, it was their holy duty to take any measures necessary to expose, punish, and uproot it, thereby restoring Israel to the benevolent graces of Yahweh.

Beside the established priesthood, there existed the *prophets*, who claimed to have received special divine revelations. The prophets often had such revelations during induced states of frenzy or ecstasy. But they vowed that these states were strictly divine in origin, unlike the drug-induced frenzies during which many diviners, magicians, and shamans claimed religious insight, especially with respect to omens and oracles. The prophets who are familiar figures in the Old Testament were usually nonprofessionals who claimed special knowledge and a divinely ordained mission to pass it on to God's community. Often *teachers*, *seers*, and *philosophers*, they were a highly respected lot and frequently held regular positions in the temple.

There was yet another class of prophets. They were the professionals, who would foretell the future or offer political or military advice for a fee. They did not enjoy the same prestige and were frequently maligned as false prophets and deceivers. They were often strongly suspected of practicing magic and divination, like the pagan priests and shamans, and on occasion were shunned by the community.

The "true" prophets were not always popular, though they might be respected. They preached whatever they were inspired to preach, even though it might be in sharp contrast to the orthodox teachings of the priests. Sometimes they condemned high-ranking public and church officials for violating the Israelites' special covenant (agreement) with Yahweh; sometimes they charged them with immoral or at least misguided behavior. The orthodox priests might answer such accusations by calling someone a false prophet, blind to the true designs of God. These sorts of feuds were not uncommon, yet the prophets played a significant role in counterbalancing—through constructive, well-intentioned, and quite often well-taken criticism—the widespread power of established priesthood. The long tradition of critical and inspirational prophecy continually challenged the temple priests to be responsive to the needs of the community, and mindful of their holy mission and heritage.

It was this deep strength and intense mission that held the Jewish people together through their humiliating Babylonian Captivity, during which they were enslaved by the Babylonians and torn away from their Holy Land and the Temple at Jerusalem. It was largely through the determination and faith of the priests—carrying out their long-held role as community leaders—that the Jews were able to survive those long years during the sixth century B.C. with a growing sense of purpose. They initiated the practice of delivering sermons to the congregations that had gathered for informal Sabbath-day meetings. In addition to sermons, the priests read from the Holy Scriptures and taught worshippers the significance of their lot as God's specially "chosen people."

The Jewish scribe-priests emphasized the legal and moral obligations and restrictions that the Jews had to follow if they were to regain God's grace. (The priests felt that the Jews' capture by the pagan Babylonians resulted because those laws had been disobeyed—and God's grace had been lost.) These laws were found in the *Torah*

*In this woodcut from the life of the Virgin Mary, a high priest rejects the offering of Joachim. (By Albrecht Dürer, early 16th century)*

and other sacred writings as well as in patriarchal traditions. The Sabbath-day meeting dealt extensively with the legal code of Moses, readings from the prophets, stories of the Jews' exodus from Egypt, and so forth.

At the new Sabbath gatherings, there was little or no room for actual liturgies and ceremonial rites, such as those that had preoccupied the priests officiating at temple services. It was an entirely different role for the priesthood—that of teacher, more than conductor of ceremonies. This type of worshipping was so far removed from the older, more formal rituals that even the meeting halls were called by a different name—not temple but *synagogue*, meaning simply "assembly." When the Babylonian Captivity ended and Jews were free to return to the Temple of Jerusalem, the synagogue did not die. It has remained a central focus of Jewish life the world over to this day. Its institution greatly expanded the scope of the priesthood, making it immediately responsive to the emotional and intellectual, as well as religious, needs of the people.

In the same period, the hierarchy of priests was also revised. The high priest was still the priest of the Temple of Jerusalem. Supposedly descended from Aaron, brother of Moses, he was, as always, the leader of both church and state. Temple ceremonies and rites were administered by the ordained priests. The Levites, as temple servants or *servitors*, tended to the property and holdings of the temple, admitted worshippers, and provided music. The newest and perhaps most important faction of priests were the *sopherim*; these priestly scribes took on the critical task of copying and interpreting the *Torah* and other sacred writings. They preserved much of the preliterary tradition of Judaism, which had previously been handed down through the generations in oral form. Moreover, they recorded the oral teachings of the poets and prophets, which might otherwise have been washed away by the tide of time.

A special group of sopherim were the *rabbis*, who taught in the synagogues much like teachers. The rabbis established village worship as a regular feature of Judaism. This not only relieved the temple of some of the burden of serving the entire community, but also permitted worship to become less formal, more instructional, and more accessible to congregational participation. The rabbis were, first and foremost, professional scribes. They served an essential function by copying the sacred books for posterity. Others were *singers* and *chanters* who also composed new works. Some rabbis helped work on the *Book of Psalms* and the *Song of Songs* as well as other poetic chants and verses.

The *Pharisees*—a priestly clan that evolved from the sopherim—acted as religious scribes some time later than the sopherim. They emphasized the legal code of the sacred books nearly to the exclusion of the rest of their rich poetic, philosophical, and prophetic tradition. In the second and first centuries B.C., they formed highly respected *schools of expounders*, which turned the Mosaic law inside out trying to capture its total essence, and to be sure that the Jewish community was living up to the holy covenant. Concerning the Scriptures, the Pharisees believed they should follow the instructions of the earlier scribes who had routinely exhorted: "Turn it and turn it again, for everything is in it." The problem was that other priests, scribes, and prophets turned it in different directions than the Pharisees thought they should, and there arose contrasting interpretations of just what the covenant was.

The priests and the sacred Scriptures formed the central focus of Jewish life. As different traditions developed within the priesthood, there was increasing conflict and animosity about which was the most appropriate way to interpret the scriptures and to minister to Yahweh's chosen people. The Pharisaic school continued to insist on a strictly legalistic interpretation of the Scriptures. The priests of this tradition saw themselves as the moral and civil overseers of the theocratic state. They were relentless in spelling out for their congregations the civil, dietary, purification, and moral laws that they discerned in their religious records and traditions. The *Sadduccees* were an elite and wealthy priesthood opposed to the Pharisees on many points. They accepted the authority of the written scriptures, but not that of oral tradition. This and many other differences between the two priestly factions ultimately led to outright violence. Only the occupation by Roman troops in 63 B.C. restored peace to a state torn by civil war. From that time on, the priests and rabbis had to face the problems of Roman rule, of repairing rifts within the Jewish community itself, and of the rising popularity of a messianic heretic who they thought lacked respect for the Mosaic law—Jesus Christ.

## Early Christianity

The Jews as well as the Romans were upset by Jesus's claims to be the Jewish messiah. Yet Jesus's famous temple debates with the Pharisees won him wide recognition as one who was well-versed in the Mosaic legal code. The Pharisees were understandably annoyed by this young upstart who—after the priesthood's centuries of severe scrutiny over every syllable and inference of Jewish law—insisted that too much fuss had been made over the law. When, on top of that, he presented himself as the prophesied messiah of the Old Testament, it was easy for the orthodox and conservative priests to declare him a madman, a heretic, or both. The Romans, meanwhile, were anxious to be rid of this radical, who boldly denounced the paganism that represented the official state religion, and whose notions of morality and service to God seemed to threaten the political security of the state.

After Jesus had been tried, convicted, and crucified for his alleged crimes, no one was left to preach his message and to witness his mission save the 12 *apostles*, or *disciples*, whom he had hand-picked for the purpose before his death. The apostles formed the nucleus of the early Christian Church, and during the first century (the so-called Apostolic Age) after Jesus's death and supposed resurrection, they set about creating a hierarchy to officiate it. As the church's original priests, the apostles and their followers conducted two basic types of worship services. First, there were the traditional synagogue-style meetings, in which there were readings, prayers, singing, and group discussions. The second type was the *agape*, or "love feast," meeting. While the former services were open to the public, the latter were restricted to true Christian believers only. The love feasts were deeply emotional gatherings during which those in attendance shared emotional reports and stories of how Christ's love had infiltrated their lives, dreams, and visions. Some spoke of divine revelations and others—while in fits of ecstasy—spoke in strange tongues believed to be divine. Most important, though, the agape was a community meal ceremoniously recalling the Last Supper, when Jesus symbolically sacrificed his blood (wine for the meal) and body (bread for the meal) for the salvation of those who believed in him. All who partook of the ceremonial bread and wine were therefore sharing in the blood and body of Christ. The priests who administered this sacred *communion* rite were obviously acting as intermediaries between man and God. Just how powerful a role this would become will be discussed shortly.

During the Apostolic Age, a priestly hierarchy began to emerge. Initially, it was quite informal. In the early Sunday morning service, during the time when Christianity was still something of an outlaw cult within the mighty Roman Empire, an unofficial leadership—actually more of a sponsorship—arose. At meetings held variously at someone's house or in a meadow, *readers*, *deacons*, and a *president* performed tasks in leading the worship that were soon taken over by an established priesthood.

One of the earliest needs for priests was to instruct prospective church members in the teachings of Christ and the workings of the church. This educational training was what came to be called the *catechism* (meaning "to instruct"). It climaxed with the ceremonious *baptism*, a spiritual purification and "rebirth" into the Christian way of salvation. While the instruction itself might have

*Jesus Christ is talking with religious scholars in the temple. (By Albrecht Dürer, early 16th century)*

been undertaken by lay persons, the baptism had to be administered by specially ordained holy men, or *priests*. The priests taught strangers the meaning of Christianity and initiated *proselytes* (converts) into the church through baptism. Soon they were also given the chore of presiding over the increasingly formal and better-organized Sunday worship meetings. A Board of Elders, or *Presbyters*, was selected to handle the administrative and organizational work of the growing church. They were supervised by a *bishop* ("overseer"), who in turn was instructed by a *deacon* (meaning "servant"). Prophets and teachers generally handled the direct instructional chores, such as delivering sermons and readings to the congregation, as well as taking over the responsibilities for catechization.

The early Christian Church gave scant heed to the work of the prophets and teachers. Many were un-ordained, but some were only wandering *evangelists* or *preachers*. The most proper work of the priesthood was thought to be officiating at ceremonies and administering the sacraments. With time, however, the church began to be much more aggressive about reaching potential converts and in spreading the word of their Christ throughout the pagan world. This tradition of proselytizing had its roots in the mission of St. Paul, himself a convert to Christianity. Paul had emphasized that Jesus was not the messiah of Israel alone but of all humanity. Many high-ranking church officials and apparently some of Jesus's own disciples opposed this broad interpretation of Christ's mission, preferring to think that the Israelites alone could be saved by his grace.

By the second century A.D., though, the Christian Church had clearly fallen in line with the thinking of Paul, the Apostle to the Gentiles. Accordingly, the preaching of sermons and the delivery and interpretation of readings became ever more significant and influential. As the Christian Church reached out to the world, preaching and teaching the word of the Lord became the most important part of the priest's job. No longer left to wandering evangelists and prophets, it was taken over by a highly organized, well-trained and ordained priesthood.

By the middle of the second century, the Christian Church had come to be referred to as *catholic*—that is, universal, rather than national or cultic. An orthodox doctrine was worked out by the elders and colleges of bishops. A strict religious organization was also created, based on the doctrine of apostolic succession. By the tenets of this doctrine, the Catholic Church claimed that all of its bishops were descendants of the Apostle Peter, Christ's first disciple. The succession had been passed on miraculously through the "laying on of hands," administered initially by Peter to his delegated followers, or bishops, and from them to the bishops that they so chose to ordain, and so forth. Every Catholic bishop, then, was considered a member of God's divine priesthood, ordained by the holy powers of the laying on of hands, administered by his immediate predecessors. Moreover, from that day to this the Catholic Church would always claim a special status for their bishops. Being descended not only from an original disciple of Jesus but from Peter, the first disciple, supposedly granted them a divine authority that no subsequent orders of bishops or priests could contest.

By 394 A.D., Christianity had become the official religion of the Roman Empire. Following centuries of persecution, Catholic bishops and priests were now the recognized establishment, as the colleges of pagan priests were dissolved. It was hoped that the monotheism (belief in God) that they represented would hold together the crumbling Roman Empire. Although the church's prestige was not quite that awesome, it had considerable effect. Christianity penetrated every aspect of Roman life, and its priesthood rose to an unparalleled status of dignity and authority. All the main churches had bishops who preached, arranged services, administered the sacraments, officiated rites and ceremonies, and ordained priests and orders of priestly *brotherhoods* and *sisterhoods*.

The bishops themselves were consecrated by the *archbishop* (also called a *primate* or *metropolitan*) and two other bishops. Their *see* (holy throne) was located in their cathedral, and they were adorned in ceremonious costumes which added grandeur to their office. Their miters (tall, peaked headgear) and pastoral staffs reminded their worshipping "flocks" that they were holy shepherds. The crosses they wore attested to their willingness to suffer for their beliefs, as they believed that Jesus had allowed himself to be crucified for the sins of all humans. Their sacred rings symbolized the holiness of their office—their spiritual "wedding" to the Lord. The chief of archbishops and bishops, and the head of the Catholic Church, was the *Pope*, who officiated at the church's headquarters in the Vatican at Rome. While the Pope's religious authority was considerable in the early years of the church, his political influence was only a shadow of what it would ultimately become after the breakup of the Roman Empire.

The fall of the empire brought an end to most of the cultural institutions of Rome. The Catholic Church survived, since a great many of the "barbarians" who took part in the destruction of Rome had previously become Christian converts themselves—or did so soon afterward. As Western Europe was plunged into a long, dark age of political disunity, along with cultural and economic stagnation, the Catholic priesthood retreated to the safety and security of the *monastery*—the one place where intellectual and cultural activities were allowed to survive. The church retained a more active role in the Eastern Roman Empire, centered on Byzantium (Constantinople, today Istanbul). There papal authority was challenged, and the Byzantine Patriarch, not the Roman Catholic Pope, was considered the head. Still, the grand era of the church's influence and power was some centuries away.

## Changes in the East

In the meantime, the priesthood continued to undergo modification in the East. The Brahmins still monopolized the priestly profession in Hinduism as a hereditary caste. Having lost some prestige to the Buddhist gurus and monks, they began to respond to the popular demand for temple-cult worship. Many of the temple priests—much less respected than the officiators of ceremonies—earned extra income by practicing astrology, fortune-telling, and divination as a private enterprise. They often served as village medicine-men as an adjunct to their priestly affairs. Many became teachers and private tutors. As scholars, they helped to copy and preserve sacred writings and also passed on both sacred and secular literature and oral traditions. Their efforts became central to the transmission of the rich cultural life that the Indians had learned to cherish. The deeper religious and philosophical teachings and scholarship remained the special province of the elite higher priesthood, however. In time, many Brahmins began entering secular professions—especially law—before taking up their true callings. So many began their professional lives as civil servants, in fact, that the lofty status of the Brahmin caste began to suffer.

While the Brahmins who performed the sacred Vedic rituals and produced enlightened philosophical treatises remained a highly prestigious lot, the increasing complexity of their performances and duties, along with what appeared to be an emotional sterility, allowed other priesthoods entirely outside of the hereditary caste to come to the fore. The gurus and ascetic "teachers" of Hinduism, Buddhism, Taoism, and other religions built reputations as great spiritual leaders without any special priestly credentials. This was especially true of the ascetic overseers of the highly emotional *bhakti* cults of the Middle Ages. They concentrated on becoming physically and spiritually overwhelmed by the love and rapture of the divine and left little room for formal ceremony or ritual. A Lingayat priesthood known as the *jangamas* practiced outside of the formally ordained priesthood, as did many other priestly and especially monastic orders. These priesthoods agreed that salvation came through individual efforts and personal enlightenment, and that the Vedic or other rituals and ceremonies—while possibly helpful towards those ends—were certainly not necessary or even always desirable. They exhorted the seeker of truth to leave behind the vain comforts of established religion, and to live the life of the ascetic while seeking the wisdom and advice of the sages and gurus.

In China, *Taoism* had become an important religion but, like Confucianism, it did not have an organized priesthood. Shamans and diviners were leaders of the various Tao cults, but their occupations were not centralized or standardized. Most lived in secular quarters with their families. They wore no special costume except during ritual performances and frequently supported themselves by selling sacred or charmed trinkets, by telling fortunes, or by casting spells against evil spirits as they wandered from village to village in search of those desiring their services. The more established and sedentary ones practiced alchemy (the attempt to make

*From India, Buddhism spread eastward, and temples like this one at Canton were found across the continent. (From* The New America and the Far East, *by G. Waldo Browne, 1901)*

gold and silver out of more ordinary metals) and astrology as part of their priestly functions. Most Tao priests claimed to be divine incarnations and, as such, could supposedly perform such wondrous feats as becoming invisible, changing mortal shapes, conferring immortality, and even walking on water. They insisted on no special or standard doctrines but generally taught such things as proper breathing techniques and dietary habits as part of secret seminar-type services, which they held periodically or by public demand.

The central feature of such services or meetings was ritualistic drumbeating accompanied by singing and gymnastics, the performers frequently being priests themselves. The most important part of the ceremonies was often done in utter silence, the idea being that the priests had special knowledge and insight that could not be properly understood by lay people. Rather than confuse them with words, which were not capable of expressing the profundity of the experience or could easily be misunderstood, the priests assumed holy postures and performed ritualistic movements that they believed could—in an unconscious way—relate the essential core of their spiritual awareness.

The notion that priests had special secrets too profound to share with lay people is not a uniquely Taoist feature. The Brahmins had copied the *Vedas* only in Sanskrit—an ancient language that few people in the general population could understand; the Zoroastrians wrote over half of their sacred *Avesta* in a dead language, which only special training could render intelligible; Catholic priests have used archaic Latin as the ceremonial language of many of their rites and ceremonies, even though many worshippers did not understand what was being said; and many leaders believed to be divinely inspired in Christianity throughout the centuries have spoken "in tongues"—nonintelligible sounds, even nonlanguage—which they alone could properly interpret.

In Japan, the *Shinto* priesthood developed into a sort of civil service position, which had close imperial ties. Almost exclusively hereditary, it was tightly organized within a strict hierarchical structure. The *Nakatomi* (ritualists) performed the important sacred rites and were the high priests of the religion. They enjoyed considerable political influence and were members of the imperial clan. The *Imbe* (abstainers) were in charge of sacrifices to the gods and were obliged to be in perfectly pure states of body and mind at the time of their ritual performances. They also helped to construct shrines dedicated to the gods. The *Urabe* (diviners) read omens and future events by studying the shape of a deer's shoulder blade, the markings of a tortoise shell, or other natural signs. The *Sarume* (musicians and dancers) helped to recite prayers and perform ritual choreographies. The *Kannushi* were the priests who tended to the daily administration as well as the religious rites and physical maintenance of the temple. They were more highly esteemed than Eastern temple-priests usually were. At one time the emperor himself had the honor of being the chief Kannushi. As community leaders, the Kannushi helped lay people with all of their personal as well as spiritual problems. They were, as a rule, quite well rewarded for their interventions with the spirit world on behalf of their reverent worshippers.

In Tibet, a monastic form of Buddhism prevailed during a time when many Buddhist monks elsewhere in Asia were finding it necessary to leave their spiritual retreats and serve temples for lay people. Tibetan monks, under the leadership of their holy superior, the *Lama*, performed priestly duties in private households but otherwise excluded themselves from such common activities. Between the eighth and thirteenth centuries A.D., the monks practiced their religious devotions largely on the fringes of society or behind monastery walls. Foreign rulers trying to centralize their authority decided to harness the mystical awesomeness of these monks for their political purposes. In 1261 A.D., Kublai Khan attempted to create a formal priesthood with the *Kuo-Shih* (instructor of the nation) at the head of the hierarchy. The experiment was a failure, though, and (until the late 20th century, when Communist China largely disbanded them) the Tibetan priesthood existed mostly in monasteries, while ministering to the community through temple and household services.

From about the fourth century A.D. to modern times, most of the Tibetan priesthood took many features of both Buddhism and Hinduism and incorporated them into a unique ritualistic form known as *Tantrism*. The Tantric priest practiced magic during public ceremonies, along with yoga breathing and exercises intended to help the pious to experience Vedic ritual as inner and personal religious experiences rather than formal ceremony.

Tantric rites were conducted in a sacred circle, the *mandala*. This became the symbol for the *prayer wheels*, which many Tibetan priests manufactured and sold throughout the villages. Sacred words (*mantras*) and symbolic hand positions (*mudras*) were used for "actual contact with the gods." Their use represented a fine magical art perfected only after long and intense training by true gurus—that is, those believed to be divine incarnates. The Tantric priest was a magician, a demonologist, a spellmaker, an exorcist, and a divine intermediate. Few priests before or since have commanded such awe from their followers, and their success had a considerable effect on making other Eastern priesthoods more responsive to lay people's desires to internalize and experience the sacred.

In the midst of these and other grand religious movements, the Brahmins joined in the new trend toward participation by lay people. As professional priests, they retained their distinctive dress codes, their shaven heads, and their celibacy policy, but they were flexible and open-minded in terms of their professional role in the world. During the Middle Ages, they built temples where people could gather to worship divine images; they developed a calendar of festivals and pilgrimages to bolster active involvement by large groups of people at one time. Those tending to the temples assumed the pastoral duties that had always been shunned by the scholarly and elite priests: officiating at marriage, birth, and death ceremonies, and at *pujas*, domestic rites in which household deities were honored.

The Brahmins' toleration of other religions and ideas was probably due mostly to the fact that they did not have to conform to the dictates of a central authority. Each priestly order and temple staff operated independently in terms of administration and precise doctrine. There were no rules and regulations or static dogmas imposed on them by a chief policy-making body. Thus they were not scolded when they came to accept three "Ways of Salvation" (good works, knowledge, and devotion) and four "Goals in Life" (pleasure, power and wealth, moral behavior, and salvation). They did not agree that these were all equally good routes to take, but felt that all were understandable and legitimate in helping individuals to higher and higher goals through the appropriate chain of rebirths—that is, through reincarnation.

## The Druids

In the Western world, Christianity was the main, but not the only, religion. Pagan cults survived for many years alongside of Christianity, particularly in northern and northwestern Europe, especially Gaul (France) and the British Isles. The most interesting priesthood among these cults was the Celtic *Druids*, about which there has been much speculation but little substantiation. The ancient Romans spoke of their wild, raving women dressed in black gowns. These women constituted the sect responsible for divination, exorcism, magic, and apparently even sorcery. The Druids offered human sacrifices to the gods, a practice that was shocking even to the Romans. Convicted murderers were reportedly sacrificed in masses, by having stakes driven through their heads or being burned in ceremonial fires.

## Islam

Before Christianity had gained a solid foothold in the Western world, *Islam* arose to challenge it. The Moslem priesthood has been strongly militant and dogmatic throughout history, following the lead of its founder, Mohammed. Upon his death in 632 A.D. Mohammed's political rulership was passed on to the *caliph* (successor). The two main branches of Islam—the majority Sunnis (meaning "orthodox") and the minority Shiites—differ in the way the succession took place. Their differences have sharpened over the years and have led to major confrontations in modern times.

Originally the caliph had been used to lead prayer sessions when the Prophet (Mohammed) was unavailable. After 632, though, the office took on the responsibility of complete political leadership. Sworn to protect (but not lead in any religious sense) the Islamic faith, the caliphate was not a religious office but a secular one. Throughout Islamic history, other political leaders have taken over virtually total religious authority for the community—the *ayatollah* being the most recent example of this.

Islam represents a curious blend of political and religious forces; the two are virtually indistinguishable in the offices and responsibilities of Moslem leaders. (The word *Moslem* means "believer" or "convert.") This has been partly due to the aggressive nature of Islam, and its self-ordained destiny to conquer and engulf new territories, to spread the holy faith. Other than the political-religious leadership at the head of Moslem society, there never has been a true Moslem religious profession.

Day-to-day religious leadership is concentrated in religious courts rather than the mosques (places of worship). The True Way or the Law (*Shari'a*) of Islam has been carefully upheld in these courts. The *ulamā* (the learned) are a conservative group of religious lawyers who, over the centuries, have taken it upon themselves to interpret Islamic law (which includes an approved body of tradition called the *Hadīth*), and to oversee the moral lives of the Moslem community.

For all the political and legal trappings of Islam, there has existed no actual priesthood to administer to worshippers, at the mosques or elsewhere. *Muezzins*, selected for their attractive and far-reaching voices, were employed to call the faithful to worship five times a day (a function largely taken over in the 20th century by loudspeakers). The ulamā have acted in the priestly tradition in terms of instructing others in the proper way of interpreting and conducting their lives according to the law. But while the ulamā have sometimes been salaried professionals, they have never constituted an ordained priesthood and have never been given the responsibility of conducting worship or presiding over sacred rites. These functions have fallen mostly to the *imam* (leader), who leads the mosque congregation in ritual, prayer, and worship of Allah—the one true God of the Moslems.

Even the imams, though, have never constituted a formal religious order. They are lay leaders of worship—either part time or full time—who have at times acted in professional capacities but never as ordained or sacred priests. Similarly, the Friday sermon (*Khutba*) has traditionally been preached by the *khatib*, who is neither

*The muezzin called the Islamic faithful to prayer from a tower called a minaret. (From* History of Egypt, *by Clara Erskine Clement)*

priest nor guru, but rather a lay community leader—sometimes a religious leader but not actually a priest.

The closest thing to a priesthood in the history of Islam has been the ecstatic *dervishes*. They were much like the Tantric priests in their use of magic and miraculous feats of accomplishment, like swallowing fire and walking on hot coals. The mystical *Sufis* also formed special religious followings, which attempted to reach the spiritual and emotional depths of Islam, speaking to those who were discontented with its highly legalistic and political overtones. They might better be considered as monks, though, as the dervishes are best regarded as ascetics. Neither group has formed ordained priesthoods.

The hierarchical structure of most of the world's religions has not really changed significantly from early medieval times to the present day. Nor has the professional priesthood changed considerably in structure or formal responsibility. But in some cases, the role of the priest in society has been altered dramatically. Nowhere is this more evident than in the case of Christianity—the dominant religion of Western civilization, that part of the world in which science, technology, commerce, and industrialization have changed human culture more rapidly and profoundly than anywhere else.

## Medieval Christianity

In the Christian West, the Roman Catholic priesthood steadily increased its power and authority in the centuries following the fall of Rome in the fifth century. Christian Europe had little centralization—political, cultural, or social. States and nations barely existed; most people lived on small feudal estates and were bound to serve petty landlords who acted as the supreme civil authorities. Warfare was nearly constant and commerce almost totally absent, so that little cultural exchange took place between isolated castle-kingdoms. Travel and communication were so poor that people only 10 or 20 miles apart might hardly be aware of each other's existence.

The priesthood, representing the Catholic Church, stood alone as a centralizing force in a world so divided. As a result, Catholic priests gained enormous prestige, power, wealth, and respect.

The medieval priesthood established Christianity as the greatest single force and feature of European life. Bishops and priests established parishes throughout the West, converting heathens. The good news of the Lord often came at the point of a sword. Charlemagne, for example, brought Christianity to the German peoples when he formed his European empire in the eighth century A.D. Scandinavians and Germans forced Christianity on many peoples of eastern Europe—in Prussia killing many hundreds of Slavs in the process.

Once established, the church played an important role in civilizing the "barbarians." The parish priest was bound to an endless round of duties. He was the *confessor*, who heard repentances for sins; the *pardoner*, who officially accepted repentances and granted indulgences in the name of the Holy Church; he was the head *cantor*, or singer of liturgies, chants, and hymns, and sometimes

*For most communicants in the Christian Church, priests were the direct representative of their religion. (By Jost Amman, from* The Book of Trades, *late 16th century)*

the parish *carilloneur* (bell ringer); he was the *verger*, who cared for the interior of the church or cathedral, and the *sexton*, who cared for the grounds and dug the graves; he was the chief *instructor* at the parish school; and he was frequently the community *healer* and personal *counselor* as well.

In the larger parishes, cathedrals, and holy sees (the bishop's office), specialists carried out these various duties, frequently under the administration of a chief bishop. Different priests were assigned to different duties, and even to special segments of society. Some were instructors in cathedral grammar schools, for instance, where the main subject was prayers and hymns. These had to be learned, recited, and chanted on a regular basis to important patrons of the church, who were thereby accorded the special grace of God. Other priests were assigned, meanwhile, to teach in the great universities, which were being founded in the 12th and 13th centuries A.D. by the church and by private donors, generally for religious purposes. The jobs of these priest-teachers were more scholastic: the teaching of Latin, public speaking, and debate—and, of course, theology.

The priesthood influenced every major and minor aspect of political, social, and economic life. It blessed and received the blessings of the established political orders, and often acted as the most powerful political force in Europe. The Holy Roman Emperor, for example, was crowned by the Pope, while much of the land in the Holy Roman Empire was held by the church and directly ruled by archbishops.

The political power of the priest came from several sources. Most obviously, he offered special prayers and therefore protection for secular authorities. He was not the magician, oracle, or diviner of the ancient religions. He was not credited with the power to cast evil spells on an enemy, confer with dead spirits, or learn through the study of astrological charts how God might respond to an attack on a neighboring kingdom. He was, however, seen as a powerful medium of divine will and grace, an intermediary between man and God. As such, he—and he alone—could plead an individual's or a ruler's case with God and possibly receive favorable judgment or intervention.

The most persuasive tool of the priests, though, became the mass. In it, they upheld the virtues of both Christianity and the established social and political order as one and the same. It was there that the priests' solid relationship with the secular authorities lay.

A widely held view in these times was that of the divine order of things, or the "Great Chain of Being." According to this concept, all of society is structured like a chain, with each individual a link. The chain was forged by God, since in His infinite wisdom, He alone could know where each and every person belonged in the order. So to attempt to change one's station in life—through economic betterment, the attainment of political power, or social improvement—was to try to improve on the social order created and ordained by God. The church strongly supported this view and at times denied the mass to people who tried to overturn the established order.

Though its power varied, the Catholic Church became the greatest central authority in the Western world, and its priests acted as its chief *diplomats* and *administrators*. The Pope assumed a major role in the selection of state as well as church leaders, beginning with the reign of Charlemagne in the eighth century A.D. And he was the guiding light of the great Crusades, in which Christian military units were gathered from all over the West in the ultimately vain attempt to recapture the Holy Land from the Moslems.

Catholic priests were highly esteemed, and the clerical profession held highly prized offices. In fact, the clerical profession represented one of the most enviable occupations of aristocratic society from the Renaissance until the 19th century. With close links to the great patrons and courtiers of European society, the priesthood offered a fine opportunity for young noblemen to attain prestigious and profitable offices. Clerical offices frequently had considerable political influence, and shrewd, industrious clergymen were often promoted into powerful and lucrative secular positions. Many of the small states, or *duchies*, that made up the Holy Roman Empire of the German people were actually ruled by Catholic archbishops, for example. Women were not permitted into the priesthood, although many became *nuns*, who worked as assistants to priests in various capacities.

The priesthood offered secure and substantial employment in a world where one could shape an honorable career only out of a court, military, or church life. For the most part, aristocrats alone had a good chance to attain high offices in the church. Even then, the church was often not a first choice, for court and military careers were considered more prestigious and attractive. Still, the priesthood offered considerable financial rewards and ample opportunity for advancement. Some priests became notoriously wealthy by selling church and professional favors. *Indulgences*, the most controversial and notable of these, were documents sold to an individual to reduce or eliminate his potential wait in Purgatory before being advanced to Heaven. The idea was in accordance with the church's notion that one could attain divine favors through the mediation of holy ordained priests. In practice, it led to substantial abuses of office, which did not always go unnoticed by parishioners.

In fact, the church was frequently criticized for its accumulation of enormous wealth, while preaching the sanctity of the poverty of the masses. Well before the Reformation such incidents as the following occurred: In 1058 the artisans (including even the well-to-do *weavers*) of one Italian state rebelled against the gaudy wealth of the priests and the worldliness of the bishops. About 50 years later, the Low Countries decreed that sacraments administered by Simoniac priests (those who bought and sold religious preferments) and married priests were invalid. And in 1143, the commune of Rome itself demanded church reforms, including more modesty in the lifestyles and earnings of the priests. The pope turned a deaf ear to such complaints, and in the last case brutally quashed the protesters with military force, executing one of its chief leaders as a heretic.

*The supreme leader of the Roman Catholic Church, the Pope is selected from among the cardinals. (By Jost Amman, from* The Book of Trades, *late 16th century)*

At the other extreme was the lowly rural *parish priest*, often called *father* or *parson* because of his paternal relations with the community that he served. This office was neither lucrative nor terribly prestigious, being held by men who were poorly trained and often largely illiterate. Erasmus—himself a churchman—must have been thinking of these men when he declared: "Among the whole batch of priests there are scarce two or three tolerable persons, and many are scarce fit for the plough-tail." Yet their influence was as profound and widespread in rural areas as that of the higher, more sophisticated clergy in the towns and universities.

Catholic priests performed mostly ceremonial tasks of religious worship. Sometimes they delivered short sermons in the vernacular (popular spoken language), but the *themas* (text readings from the Bible) were always given in Latin. This added to the mystique of their holy office, as did their rituals and their somber administration of the sacraments. They were surrounded by austere statues of the saints and holy relics, and carried themselves with grandeur. Their celibacy was supposed to make them pure and their very ordination (the ceremony at which they became priests) was believed to have made them messengers of God. For centuries—and even to this day—many Catholics have revered these men as the closest thing to a link between mortals and God. In a world possessed with a fear (partly instilled by the church itself) of demons and the wrath of God, the figure of the priest was one of comfort, stability, and assurance that all difficulties and trials had a divine and ultimately benign purpose.

## The Protestant Reformation

Another type of Christian priesthood arose in the 16th century. Protestant reformers of the Catholic Church argued that no mortals were ordained as God's envoys or mouthpieces; that priests had no authority to hear people's confessions of sin or to pardon them; that they ought not to be celibate because God bade man to replenish the Earth with his offspring and to take a woman to avert the illicit temptations of carnal lust; and that they certainly could not sell guarantees of certain divine actions or judgments (the sale of indulgences being a major issue in the establishment of Protestantism). Beyond this, the Protestants complained about the worldliness of the priesthood, of its preference for political and economic concerns rather than spiritual ones. The bloody violence that resulted in the establishment of Protestant sects was part of what is known as the *Reformation*.

These new reformed sects aspired to a simpler religious life. Its ministers were trained to be teachers and educators primarily, since their main role was to lead their congregations in reading (for themselves) and interpreting (with strict guidance) the Holy Scriptures. Ritual had little place in Protestant churches; the veneration of saints had none. The prayer halls were simple. Some had none at all, but worshipped in their homes instead, often without any formal ministers. The ministers were community leaders who did not aspire to great wealth, prestige, or political power. At least, that was the theory. In fact, some of the Protestant ministers later attained great power and obtained considerable wealth.

The early Protestant ministers gained great influence through sermons. Preached in the vernacular—that is, in the popular language, rather than in Latin—the sermons were designed to guide the behavior of a nearly or actually theocratic community—that is, one governed by church officials claiming divine authority. John Calvin, one of the early Protestant leaders, ruled over a theocratic government in Geneva, where he warned people in his carefully outlined sermons how their lives ought to be lived to the most minute detail: what time they should go to bed, how to spend their leisure time (the few hours between dinner and bedtime), and even what things should not be thought or dreamt about. There were strict, sometimes severe, punishments for overt offenses against the "government of God" created by the church ministers and elders.

*Calvinism* was not the only example of such austerity and harshness. The *Puritans* who settled the American Colonies also attempted to set up a theocracy. Their ministers preached that they were not escaping from persecution in Europe so much as they were embarking on a divinely commissioned "errand into the wilderness" to establish a "city on a hill." Puritan ministers believed that the American wilderness was where they were being led by God, just as the Jews had been led into the desert wilderness after their deliverance from Egypt. The Aaronic priesthood had been ordained to lead the people of Moses to Israel, which would become a holy example of God's purpose and law; so the Puritan leaders were to lead their people to the "New Israel" (America), which would become a city on a hill for all observers to see. This "city" was to be founded squarely on Mosaic law and Christian principles, and a church-directed government would insure that God's "chosen people" would not be led astray. The American Colonies would be a divine settlement, a "New England," which the Old England would eventually choose to imitate.

As the Protestant churches became ingrained in the cultures and societies they intended to restructure, their ministers—especially those of second and later generations—tended to become less zealous in their theories and demands. Their influence remained profound, nonetheless, and actually helped pave the way for the Commercial and Industrial revolutions. From their pulpits and in their religious tracts, the Protestant leaders preached social and economic reform. Salvation, they believed, was bestowed on an individual by divine grace. Earthly success, many Protestant ministers believed, was a sign of that divine grace. Individuals therefore had strong reason to work hard and show that they were among God's elect. Those who prospered in life, the Protestants believed, were those who were obviously blessed; they were also people who performed good works and lived simple, industrious lives. These theories stressed the equality of all people before God. Work came to be seen as an almost sacred act.

Even before the lifetime of Martin Luther, many Europeans had come to believe that they could, indeed, alter their inherited status in life through their own hard work. After the Reformation, this idea was eagerly embraced by many Protestants. To them, the old theory that a person could not progress beyond his station through individual effort was designed to serve the interests of the Catholic Church, and of the kings and nobles who had used it for centuries to hold the masses "in their place." Because the individual's hard work was central to this idea, it has often been referred to as the "Protestant work ethic." But its importance was even wider than that, for it meant that people could actually shape their own lives and futures.

This was one of the most revolutionary ideas in the history of civilization. In the years just after Luther's break with the Catholic Church, the bloody Peasant Revolts of Germany—sparked largely by this new idea of the individual's place in the world—struck terror in the hearts of Europe's ruling classes. Not all the changes that followed would be so bloody, but changes there would be—and massive ones—throughout the Western world in the centuries that followed. A new middle class replaced the old landed gentry as leaders of the state and sponsors of the new capitalist economy. And in time, divine right monarchs themselves were replaced by democratic and representative forms of government.

The Protestant ministers did not actually direct such overwhelming events, of course. In fact, their role in history as revolutionaries has been much overplayed. As a group, they favored social stability as much as anyone, and they preached the same "Great Chain of Being" doctrines that Catholic priests did. But they also came to be more tolerant of scholarly learning and the new advances in scientific thought that the Catholic hierarchy often opposed so bitterly. They opened schools and taught many more people to read, write, and interpret. Their initial purpose was to increase Bible reading, but this soon expanded to many other areas of intellectual pursuit. Protestant universities were more likely to teach mathematics and biology, while their older Catholic counterparts moved only slowly away from their medieval obsession with *scholasticism*, nit-picking theological studies based on dogmatic assumptions.

*This scripture reader is attempting to comfort or convert those in his night refuge. (By Gustave Doré, from* London: A Pilgrimage, *1872)*

Protestant ministers were often community leaders, but as the Industrial Revolution drew nearer, their prestige dropped. They never enjoyed the central administration that Catholic priests had long had, but were broken up into countless sects. The result was that each church tended to be more or less self-sufficient and self-governing, although it did have to answer to vaguely empowered officiating councils. Many North American ministers were wanderers, officiating at services in one town one week, the next town the following week, and so forth. Others doubled as *teachers*, *tutors*, and *undertakers* to increase their meager earnings. Few church-related occupations existed outside of the ministry itself. The ministers usually tended to the bell ringing, maintained the building, and did the church-school teaching with the aid of lay volunteers.

The 19th and 20th centuries have marked great changes in the profession of priest and minister in the Christian world. The Industrial Revolution led the way to the creation of a more materialistic and leisurely society than had ever been known before—one that is still unknown to many non-Western peoples. As science and machines began to harness nature and ease disease, poverty, and famine, the world of devils and evil spirits became increasingly remote. As cities and factory work separated humans from their direct dependence on the land, the harvest, and the weather, they began to feel less vulnerable and meek. Indeed, science and industry appeared as a sort of salvation, in and of themselves. People had more and more leisure time: time for dancing, the theater, and card playing—all of which had once been considered dire vices in most Puritan towns. Automobiles and electronic devices, such as television, movies, and game machines, have given people ample diversion in free time that once might have been spent on prayer and Bible lessons. All of these radical changes in society have been coupled with an increasing materialism in overall world view. In general, the *physician*, not the priest, has become the healer; *psychologists* tend to treat people with mental disorders and criminal records, where once they may have been hunted and burned as witches or devils; *biologists* more than theologians discuss the creation of the universe and the origin of the species.

The Christian ministry and priesthood have tried to keep pace. Since the early 1800's, professional seminaries have increased their standards of training and education for prospective clergy. Still, the number of persons in the professional ranks have dropped dramatically, especially since World War II. Some blame a lack of high-quality clergy for the phenomenon that has been called the "death of the church." Certainly, with the wide range of potential careers available to people since the industrialization of society, the priesthood or ministry is no longer one of the first choices. It demands extensive schooling and training for far less income than many other careers offer. The Catholic priesthood has especially suffered, not only for the reasons mentioned, but also because of its time-honored insistence of the celibacy of its members. Large numbers of priests and nuns have left their professions in the last two decades over this policy. To fill out its thinning ranks, the Catholic Church has recently begun accepting widowers, who are becoming priests as a kind of second career in life.

Other issues have also worked against the health of the profession. Women have been excluded from ordination in the Catholic Church, and some Protestant churches are only beginning to include them. The first woman bishop of the United Methodist Church was ordained only in 1980. There has also been a good deal of controversy over the amount of social and political involvement that clergy should have, in comparison with their duties as spiritual leaders.

## Modern Cults

Generally speaking, the professional priest of today engages in a more humanistic than ritualistic service. There are many exceptions to this of course, like the hereditary Parsis, derived from the ancient Magi, and revived in the East in the latter 19th century. Like some other Eastern orders, the Parsis continue to be mostly illiterate leaders of magical rituals and sacred ceremonies.

In most of the civilized and industrialized areas of the world, the closest kin to the ancient magical, divining, and medicine-man priest are *faith healers* and *cult leaders*. These are ordained or self-professed religious leaders who claim special divine powers or knowledge to heal sickness of the mind, body, and spirit. They claim to lead an initiated group into a special and usually immediate relationship with the divine, the ultimate goal being salvation and eternal life. The initiation is usually informal, although cult leaders may require quite severe and costly initiation and membership obligations.

## Priestly Occupations

While many such cult leaders operate today, much as they did in ancient times, they are definitely exceptions to the rule in the priestly professions. For the most part, religious leaders have become more secular and less mystical in their outlook on life and in their performance of

*Along with the major religions have always come smaller sects, like these serpent-handlers of the Pentecostal Church of God, in Harlan County, Kentucky, 1946. (By Russell Lee, National Archives, Records of the Solid Fuels Administration for War, 245-MS-2621L)*

their duties. In part, this has become necessary in a materialistic and rationalistic world, where concepts of magic, spirits, and perhaps even divinity have become less tenable or realistic to many people. The various orders of priests have responded by becoming more involved in practical and earthly concerns. This behavior has, however, often made their offices even less prestigious in society. This has been particularly true in the West, where rationalism and materialism are most prominent. But even in the East, 20th-century Brahmins have had to resort to all kinds of lowly and secular part-time jobs in order to support themselves financially. In sum, fewer individuals are seeking the religious professions and many are leaving them. Those in the profession often work for less financial reward, community esteem, and job security than they previously received. Many have had to take on additional work, with jobs in teaching usually providing the most financial support and prestige.

Besides the main priestly occupations discussed to this point, countless specialties and honorary positions—both ordained and lay—have been a part of the history of this profession. Roman Catholicism, traditionally a highly ritualistic religion, has many various types and titles of personnel. Among these are the important and high-ranking *bishops*, some of whom received the honorary title of *cardinal* after the sixth century A.D. The Sacred College of Cardinals—made up purely of bishops—was a privileged class in Rome. From 1059 A.D. on it has been empowered to elect the Pope. In fact, the Pope has been chosen exclusively from among the ranks of cardinals since 769 A.D. As advisers and envoys of the Pope, cardinals gained enormous prestige and power in the medieval church and have largely retained it to this day. In 1965, the Pope began the practice of conferring this high title on Eastern patriarchs as well as Roman bishops.

*Vicar* and *legate* (meaning "substitute") are other honorary titles that have been bestowed on Catholic priests since the eighth century A.D. Vicars have sometimes acted as representatives and envoys of the

Pope. *Rector* is a title of institutional leadership as of a cathedral, university, or abbey. It has been used in a variety of ways in both Catholicism and Protestantism and is especially prominent in denoting Church of England and Episcopalian clergy. *Pastor* (meaning "shepherd") generally refers to any member of the priesthood, as does the pious title of *reverend*. Slightly higher in status than the ordinary Catholic priest is the *monsignor*. Like the terms cardinal and vicar, this is an honorary title rather than an actual office.

   *Deacons* and *deaconesses* are not priests, but have semi-priestly duties. The *diaconate* has historically been associated with ceremonial and caretaking duties. Deacons and deaconesses were originally enlisted in the service of the Christian Apostles to relieve them of routine chores so that they could be free to proselytize—try to win converts—and spread news of the Gospel. The deacons were administrative aides, while the deaconesses acted as doorkeepers to the church, tended to the sick and the poor, and were particularly useful in assisting in the baptism of women, since the female convert had to disrobe during the baptismal ceremony. In the sixth century

*This Russian priest is a member of the Eastern Orthodox branch of Christianity. (From* Peoples of the World, *19th century)*

A.D., the Roman Catholic Church abolished the office of deaconess for some time, but it grew in importance in the Eastern churches. There were also subdeacons, who assisted the deacons, and archdeacons.

All religions have had a variety of occupations attached to them, although the titles we are most familiar with are those of honor or recognized leadership within a church or sect. A *swami*, or *sadhu*, is an ascetic who is usually revered by his followers as a sort of saint, albeit an unordained spiritual leader. This title has come to be associated particularly with the Ramakrishna sect. An *ayatollah* is the recognized religious leader in Iran, as is the *lama* in Tibet. The ayatollahs' power and influence have varied over the years, reaching its height in the 20th century in the person of Khomeini. He was instrumental in the proclamation of a new constitution in 1979, which gave the Moslem clergy unprecedented privileges in Iranian society.

*Chaplains* and *missionaries* work outside the normal structure of the church hierarchy. Chaplains serve within large institutions, such as universities, hospitals, prisons, orphanages, and military bases. They usually live within these special communities and associate closely with their populations. *Military chaplains* are commissioned officers. Missionaries carry the word and faith of their religions to lands and cultures where they are largely or wholly unknown. In history, the work of the missionaries has been instrumental in the spreading of the world's great religions—particularly Christianity and Islam.

Despite the declining role of the clergy in society, there are some indications of a revival, given international relations in the nuclear age. One reason for the decline of the priestly role is that the age of industrialization, job security, and high standards of living left industrialized society reasonably secure with life and relatively unconcerned with death. Historically, the priesthood was regarded as a means of salvation in the afterlife, and good health and prosperity in this one. In the 20th century humans became increasingly concerned with this life and less sure of even the existence of the next one, while great

*In many Midwestern communities, revival meetings were—and are—an important part of life. (By Arthur Rothstein, from* The Depression Years, *Dover, 1978)*

advances in medicine and economic growth seemed to diminish the priestly role in promoting health and prosperity.

Recently, though, there has been some shift of world outlook. Despite the accomplishments of medicine, science, and technology, humanity now stands closer to mass holocaust and environmental collapse than ever before. People are increasingly becoming concerned about the end of human history in their lifetimes. Various religious leaders have become deeply committed to tackling head on the great international crises of nuclear disarmament, human rights, and environmental pollution. The Roman Catholic Pope has supported oppressed workers in Poland and an amiable settlement of civil and religious strife in war-torn Ireland. Many leaders in the other major religions have taken similar initiatives.

The *ecumenical movement*—an attempt to unite the multitude of Christian sects and churches under one generally accepted authority, philosophy, and purpose—itself floundered for many years over such issues as the authority of the Catholic, Anglican, and Episcopalian bishops, the extent of the authority of the Catholic Pope and the Orthodox Patriarch, and so forth. The immensity of the problems of interfaith and inter-religious cooperation may be seen in the Roman Catholic attitude toward heretics, which for centuries it has defined as those opposing the established hierarchy of the "one true" church (meaning the Roman Catholic Church), and those who contest the divine authority and infallibility of the Pope. By this definition, all non-Catholics are "heretics." Even today, the oath of allegiance that all Roman Catholic bishops are obliged to swear still includes this declaration: ". . . with all my power I will persecute and make war upon heretics." The clergy is at a major turning point in its history, and it is hard to predict the direction the profession will take in the future.

For related occupations in this volume, *Scholars and Priests*, see the following:
  Curators
  Librarians
  Monks and Nuns
  Scholars
  School Administrators
  Teachers

For related occupations in other volumes of the series, see the following:
in *Artists and Artisans*:
  Painters
in *Communicators*:
  Authors
  Clerks
  Scribes
in *Financiers and Traders*:
  Accountants and Bookkeepers
  Bankers and Financiers
  Merchants and Shopkeepers
  Stewards and Supervisors

in *Harvesters*:
  Beekeepers
  Farmers
  Hunters
in *Healers* (forthcoming):
  Physicians and Surgeons
  Psychologists and Psychiatrists
in *Helpers and Aides*:
  Private Guards and Detectives
  Servants and Other Domestic Laborers
  Social Workers
  Undertakers
in *Leaders and Lawyers*:
  Diplomats
  Judges
  Lawyers
  Political Leaders
in *Performers and Players*:
  Actors
  Athletes
  Dancers
  Musicians
in *Restaurateurs and Innkeepers* (forthcoming):
  Bakers and Millers
  Prostitutes
  Winemakers
in *Scientists and Technologists*:
  Alchemists
  Astrologers
  Biologists
  Geographers
  Geologists

# Scholars

Scholars have usually been associated with academic institutions, particularly those of higher education. Throughout history they have been employed because of their expertise in a particular field, in which they are expected to carry on scholarly research. Most academic scholars are not directly compensated for their research and findings, however; instead they are employed and paid as *teachers*. Here we will focus on scholars primarily as a part of the higher education teaching profession, since they are so linked with it, even though the function of teaching in their case is often secondary to those of research and writing. Other scholars earn their livings in other professions, among them those of *author*, *scientist*, and *priest*; a small number are supported by the government or private funds.

*Socrates carried out his sentence of death by drinking poison. (From* Museum of Antiquity, *by L.W. Yaggy and T.L. Haines, 1882)*

The philosophers of ancient Greece were among the earliest scholars. Many of them received gifts and patronage in return for the wisdom—usually in the form of philosophical thought—that they imparted. Socrates was the foremost of this group, but he was strongly opposed to the practice of receiving compensation or patronage for his services. He believed this to be an inherent conflict of interest, since the philosopher was duty-bound to criticize society and expose the weaknesses and contradictions embedded in the state as well as in the culture. Aristotle, on the other hand, eagerly accepted liberal patronage and sumptuous living quarters at the courts of aristocrats and tyrants, notably the emperor Alexander the Great. The status of the Greek philosophers varied with the times and according to personalities and external events. Socrates was eventually condemned to death, and both Plato and Aristotle were exiled from Greece at different times during their lives.

Scholars were hard pressed to find employment in the ancient world, except at the great libraries and museums, notably at Alexandria in Egypt. There, the generosity of the Ptolemaic rulers attracted scores of learned *writers, philosophers,* and *historians* to translate and extensively annotate the ancient texts of the Egyptians, Persians, and Babylonians, among others. As an outgrowth of this flourishing activity, a sort of textual criticism industry developed in Alexandria. Scholarship won such acclaim that the Greek rulers and other aristocrats in the Western world vied to have well known scholars reside in their courts.

Scholarship during this period was essentially of three types: historical, philosophical, and literary. *Historians* were the closest allies of the state, since they interpreted world events—past and contemporary. Often these interpretations tended to praise the existing political order and uphold the culture of the homeland. If historians gave negative interpretations, they would often have difficulty publishing them. By the time of the Roman Empire such works might lead to exile, imprisonment, or even death. Most historians, then, found it prudent to write favorably of their homeland and patrons. Since historians were the main *chroniclers* and *reporters* of contemporary events, they performed some of the work done by the modern news media. Court societies understandably found their works important enough to closely monitor and patronize—the latter function nicely serving the former.

It is hard to say where the works of the philosophers and literary figures diverged, but both fields were broad and highly respected until the later days of the Roman Empire. Most Greek and Roman courts retained *poets* and *philosophers* as a matter of status more than anything else. Philosophers were involved not only in abstract thought but also with such matters as music, athletics, and diet. The Greek gymnasiums—where men convened for games and physical conditioning—were common sites of elaborate philosophical and literary dialogues.

Informal schools tended to develop around the most prominent scholars. Socrates and the other Greek philosophers conducted loosely arranged symposia.

Plato attracted followers to his Academy and Aristotle to his Lyceum. Aristotle established himself as one of the leading *scientists* of the times by virtue of his lengthy observations and recordings of the natural world. *Astronomers*, *physicians*, *mathematicians*, and other scientists also carried on research of a scholarly nature. Although most of these scholars were men, a few of them—in Alexandria, at least—were women. Among them were the famous mathematician and philosopher Hypatia, who was killed as a pagan by a Christian mob, and Mary the Jewess, who developed the techniques of distillation.

As the Roman Empire declined, the tradition of scholarship spread eastward. Nestorian Christians, branded as heretics by the now-dominant church, fled to many areas, most notably Arabia and Persia, often bearing with them their extensive libraries of classical writings. These formed the basis for early Persian scholarship, which drew also on Indian and even some Chinese traditions as well. The fruits of this were borne in the Islamic period, a great age for scholars.

Early Islamic leaders brought to their courts the most eminent scholars of the region—Christian and Jewish as well as Moslem. These scholars gathered around them informal schools, in the Classical tradition. At first they concentrated on collecting, translating, and copying writings from the earlier Greek and Roman civilizations. Later they made original contributions in many areas, among them mathematics and astronomy, especially in the 10th and 11th centuries A.D. in Moslem Spain.

Although large numbers of scholars continued to be supported at major courts throughout the great age of Islam, many found employment in the great universities of the period, like those at Damascus, Baghdad, and Córdoba. These scholars were mostly male, but the tradition of informal home education allowed some women to become highly respected scholars.

Scholars were not invulnerable, however. As elsewhere in history, waves of anti-intellectualism led to persecution of scholars and burning of libraries at times under Moslem rule. But in general the scholarship tradition was strong. It provided the basis upon which the Renaissance of Christian Europe would later flourish.

While Greece was in its Golden Age, China was experiencing a glittering age of its own. In about the fifth century B.C., China was in the age of the Hundred Schools. Its many contending states vied with one another to attract great scholars like Confucius to their courts. Scholars were given not only professional respect and social esteem, but considerable material support as well. Eager students gathered around these many scholars, and literacy reached previously unknown heights. Rarely, if ever, have scholars been rewarded so fully for their special gifts.

Unfortunately, this age was followed by one in which all scholars except those who followed the Legalist School were in disfavor. Moreover, books of differing scholars were burned, and many scholars who refused to give up their books were put to death. Some managed to hold copies in secret hiding places, and these would later be the basis of a revival of learning.

When violent repression ended, however, freely contending schools were no longer the norm. From the third century B.C. up into modern times, Confucianism was more or less dominant in China; the extensive literature and commentary that developed around it were the cement of the Chinese state and Chinese society. Scholars were still held in high esteem, as servants of the state. The elite civil administration of the country was always drawn from among the ranks of scholars. The continuity provided by the Confucian philosophy of life made China one of the most stable societies in the world for many centuries.

Ancient Chinese society also formalized and organized scholarship far beyond any other system. Scholars had to pass competitive and relatively democratic civil service examinations to attain the title of *scholar*. This was a formal civil service position in the state administration. Countless thousands of *expectants* entered the elaborate examinations after dutiful years of training, but only a few achieved the coveted and even venerated status of scholar.

These few were privileged to wear distinctive yellow coats and colored buttons on their headdresses, signifying their special ranking. This was a far more rigid occupational arrangement than in the West, where anyone who could attract a faithful following could claim for himself the rather elusive title of scholar.

As Chinese scholars contributed to the stability of social customs and political systems through their religious and ethical teachings, so medieval Western scholars supported the conservative social, political, and religious positions of the Roman Catholic Church. Religion permeated all research and ideas, so that it not only molded secular investigation but also led to an active scholarship within established religious spheres. Priests increasingly became prominent scholars with the rise of the Christian church, dedicated as it was to making education its servant and chief witness. The church formally denounced secular (and therefore "pagan") learning. Even outstanding church fathers such as Clement, Origen, and Augustine had become leading scholars in the study of the pre-Christian world. This precedent insured that as the church became the center of cultural activity throughout the Middle Ages, the priesthood would dominate scholarship. Western scholarship was rooted in theology for many centuries. This led to the sophisticated and intricate dialogues of the *scholastics*, who adroitly joined faith and reason.

The medieval university developed in Europe coincidentally with, and as an outgrowth of, scholasticism. Originally, *university* was a term that denoted only conventions of faculty members in the most common fields and disciplines, such as theology, medicine, and law. Eventually it came to indicate the institution of higher learning. This development created a fertile environment for the professionalization of scholarship.

Later centuries saw a great increase in the number of appointments of scholarly professors and the rapid improvement in the socio-economic status of the occupation. The university grew out of a more informal learning situation known as a *studium generale*, created by the banding together of teachers and learners. The university became distinctive as a "higher" form of education by virtue of its complexity and intricately intellectual nature. Teachers were called *masters* in Paris and *doctors* in Bologna, in tribute to their considerable scholarly background in their subjects. Theology was the original and primary subject matter and so it remained well into the 19th century. Law and medicine were also noteworthy subjects, but science remained suspect in the eyes of the church authorities, who held considerable control over university curricula and the appointment of masters.

University professors used the methods of lecture and disputation. They were paid according to student enrollments and therefore conceded much to student demands. Eminent scholars like Peter Abelard and Bernard of Chartres could attract more students than they could reasonably instruct. The more common master would have to give banquets, agree to make lectures brief and stimulating, and employ other such tactics in order to sustain a tuition-paying clientele. Some beginning instructors even paid students to enter their classes to stimulate interest and appeal.

Because of the lack of books, professors had to lecture carefully and slowly. Their lectures were termed *ordinary lectures* and were usually given in the morning. *Extraordinary lectures* were given later in the day by especially quick students; these consisted of a near repetition of the master's lecture for the benefit of those who were slow at taking notes or who had fallen asleep the first time around. Professors were generally held in high esteem and were more than adequately compensated; some were actually wealthy. Most were priests from the Catholic Church. Professors taught in rather dogmatic fashion from thronelike seats, wearing glittering jewels and robes and surrounded by students clamoring for good seating space on the floor.

The *Humanists*, while usually devout clerics themselves, opened the door for a greater secularization of learning. Inspired by ancient Greece and Rome, Renaissance men like Erasmus began to call for a more fully developed learning at universities. They thought all subjects should be opened to intellectual review. Such ideas were at first considered heretical, especially where they led to scientific research and teachings that were considered at odds with the teachings of the Roman Catholic Church and the Holy Scriptures. They eventually were accepted, thanks in no small measure to the Protestant Reformation. The universities began to counter criticisms that they were impractical and therefore limited to the entertainment and whims of a small, elite, and financially secure aristocratic class. Many a university would say (as would Yale University at its founding in 1701) that it was established to train men "fitted for public employment."

The rise of science, reason, and mechanization altered the outlook of scholars and the expectations that society had of them. By the 19th century they were much less likely to be endowed with the burden of sustaining religious orthodoxy than they had been earlier; their

*Through the centuries, many scholars have earned their living by teaching at universities. (From* Frank Leslie's Popular Monthly Magazine, *19th century)*

chores had become more practical and humanitarian. They were increasingly charged with the task of improving society and the human condition, especially in light of the abuses and dehumanization of urban life that were born of the Industrial Revolution. Theology and philosophy began to take a back seat to the *social sciences*, which were supposed to make the world a better place to live, and the *natural sciences*, which were aimed at improving people's ability to manipulate the environment and harness its energies. Fewer professors had any church ties or even religious inclinations, and the decline of religious and church authority opened the way for a larger number of disciplines to find a home in the university.

The University of Halle in Germany was the first university to restrict studies within its jurisdiction to those of a purely graduate and professional nature. It did this early in the 19th century, but as early as a century before it had introduced a curriculum of advanced science and mathematics. The precedent set by this pioneer institution firmly established the university as an unparalleled institution of higher learning. Meanwhile, it clearly digressed from its ecclesiastical ties and declared the benefit of the state to be the primary challenge assigned to its scholars in residence.

When the University of Berlin was founded in the 19th century, it took pains to staff its faculties with eminent scholars and researchers and made substantial and innovative research the primary task of its professors. It soon began awarding a new degree—the doctor of philosophy (Ph.D.)—for original research written and presented as a special documented report called a *dissertation*. Since the Ph.D. was considered the proper credential for completing university instruction at Berlin, the aim was clearly to produce scholars rather than teachers. It was assumed that scholars would be good teachers purely by virtue of their mastery of specific subject matter.

Scholars became ever more important to the development of the university as the 19th century progressed. In

America, Yale became the first university to award the Ph.D., in 1861; others quickly followed. Even more important was the nature of the research that began to develop from this insistence on scholarship as a qualification for teaching in higher education. Industrialization and urbanization had led to the creation of complex cosmopolitan societies. Specialization became the order of the day. *Sociologists, psychologists, philologists,* and many other specialties all developed their own faculties. These were added to those of the *theologians, historians,* and *philosophers.* Scientists began to specialize within their departments, so that there were *astronomers, biologists, chemists,* and *physicists* rather than just "scientists." *Mathematicians* and others did likewise.

The 20th century has seen the greatest specialization of scholarship that humanity has ever known. University teachers are urged, sometimes even forced, to be scholars. "Publish or perish" has characterized university life since the end of the last century, when teachers at the University of Pennsylvania were sent packing unless they stopped "wasting" time and energy on teaching and began producing "white paper"—that is, scholarly—reports in their respective fields. Today, there are countless technical and academic journals covering every conceivable subject and specialization within it. While these publications are in print to increase the body of knowledge within a field, they also perform the important function of permitting university professors to "get published" and, therefore, to be established as scholars. Academic articles as well as dissertations sometimes seem to have no purpose or benefit to anyone other than the author who was clever enough to develop a unique angle that no one else had yet explored (or cared to). Technical language often clouds the minute size of the contribution being made.

On the other hand, a different, more recent trend in scholarship seems to be that which produces mass-appeal scholars. Paperback books and television and radio talk shows have lent themselves particularly to this phenomenon. For example, a noted psychiatrist develops a method of self-assertiveness and writes up a "how to achieve it" program in lay terminology rather than in the technical jargon of the field. It comes out in paperback, sells well, and is boosted by the public appearance of the author on a general audience television or radio talk show. Suddenly, the author is seen as an authority and a scholar in the field simply by becoming a recognizable celebrity or personality. Such a figure delivers lectures, goes on more talk shows, writes more books, and is sought after by numerous universities. The only drawback is that such a person's status as an authority is often due more to mass appeal—stemming from the speaker's "image"—than to solid and substantial documented research.

The issue of authority has been a troublesome one for scholars throughout history. If scholars' work involves serious research on a topic and produces findings that can be readily substantiated, they should easily be able to claim and receive recognition for their work as authoritative—that is, as reasonably dependable and conclusive. However, this has rarely been the case. Authority has often become a cliché and a password for orthodoxy—meaning the views held by the controlling group in a particular field. In the ancient world, tyrants and emperors in particular, and the state in general, were such orthodox and widely accepted authorities. When Socrates provided solid evidence showing that the state in some concrete ways countered the general good of society, he was criticized for his supposed ignorance, insolence, and lack of authority. Even after his statements were refined and more thoroughly substantiated, they were not accepted as more scholarly and therefore noteworthy, but were violently condemned as seditious. Socrates eventually paid for his views with his life.

In the early 17th century, Galileo completed extensive research supporting the Copernican solar system theory. In 1616 he was summoned to Rome, where Catholic Church authorities warned him to stop teaching the

Copernican system because it was contrary to church views and an obstacle to faith. But in 1632 Galileo published a work that documented solid evidence supporting Copernicus's contention that the Sun, rather than the Earth, was indeed the center of our solar system. A year later he was tried by the Roman Inquisition. This forced him to recant his scientific findings as lacking in authority—indeed, the church declared that it alone possessed intellectual authority, which was unattainable by independent scholarship. Galileo was sentenced to an enforced residence in Siena, where his research could no longer cause embarrassment to the Church or undermine its authority.

These are but two examples among thousands where scholarship was subordinated to the whims of more influential and powerful authorities. Contemporary Western scholars work in a presumably open, scientific, and democratic environment. Their views and findings are not supposed to be harnessed and reshaped by political or religious review. There remain, however, serious obstacles to scholarly freedom to pursue truly scientific and objective research. This comes mainly in the form of "authoritative" scientific and educational communities that, in turn, can sometimes behave as the handmaidens of both government and big business.

Most scholars depend on university appointments for their livelihoods, so they must contend with administrative and departmental controls. Universities have almost a stranglehold on many forms of scholarship. Independent scholars who have no academic, institutional, or professional ties have difficulty obtaining serious review of their research or theoretical papers. Yet many scholars cannot obtain appropriate appointments because they are not recognized, published authorities. As a result, those scholars who retain appointments tend to be intellectually inbred and prone to formulating views deemed worthy within their own professional circles. This development has impeded the process of impartial, objective, and visionary research. The problem is even worse in nations with totalitarian governments, where scholars must serve the goals and perceptions of the state and its highest officials.

In modern times, women have once again formally rejoined the class of scholars. Some women had always been scholars, of course, especially those who grew up in scholarly families. But only in a few times, such as in third-century B.C. Alexandria or in the convents of the Middle Ages, were their activities given much support. With the rise of the universities in Europe, they were officially excluded from formal higher education. Only in the last two centuries have women gained access to university educations and thereby obtained the credentials necessary for pursuing scholarly work.

But if much has changed, some things have not. While most scholars continue to earn their livings by teaching or related occupations, some are supported by government subsidies or by rich patrons, often today by funds channeled through foundations. Nor are scholars less vulnerable to public reaction against their work. A strik-

*As women entered higher education, many became scholars in their own right, such as Mary Emma Woolley, president of Mount Holyoke College in 1903. (By Purdy Studio, Boston Library of Congress)*

ing example of this was in the Chinese Cultural Revolution of the 1960's, in which institutions of higher education and research were closed and scholars were sent to work in the fields as part of their "re-education."

Throughout history, scholars have been much influenced by their times, if only because they earn their livings in the community at large. This pressure has led some scholars to undue conservatism and focus on details at the expense of a wider picture. But at their best, scholars are impartial seekers after truth, who perform a unique function in a world full of interested parties.

For related occupations in this volume, *Scholars and Priests*, see the following:
  Librarians
  Monks and Nuns
  Priests
  Teachers

For related occupations in other volumes of the series, see the following:
in *Communications*:
  Authors
  Editors
  Journalists and Broadcasters
  Publishers and Booksellers
  Scribes
in *Healers* (forthcoming):
  Physicians and Surgeons
in *Leaders and Lawyers*:
  Judges
  Lawyers
  Political Leaders
in *Scientists and Technologists*:
  Alchemists
  Astronomers
  Biologists
  Chemists
  Mathematicians
  Physicists

# School Administrators

Until the Middle Ages, schools were usually operated by one person or a very small group of persons. Since these people were also *teachers*, no special or separate occupation of *school administrator* was needed. Medieval schools in the Christian world were administered by a hierarchy of Catholic Church officials from the Pope down to the bishop, who was responsible for the local administration of parish and cathedral schools. The bishop often appointed a *scholasticus* to oversee day-to-day affairs in the schools. The *scholasticus* not only supervised instruction and curricular designs but even licensed teachers as well as appointing them. Universities, too, were run primarily by the church in the later Middle Ages and the Renaissance. As cities began to develop during the Renaissance, however, some of the administrative control and obligation fell into the hands of secular authorities, particularly trade and merchant guilds and city and town governments.

After the Protestant Reformation of the 16th century, the state gained considerable authority in areas that had once been exclusively in the hands of the Pope and lesser church officials. Monarchs began to assume much of the administrative control over all schools, and public officials were appointed to supervise the schools. These officials, who were especially common in the Protestant countries, acted as *supervisors* and *administrators*.

In this they followed the model of some earlier *chantry schools*. A chantry was founded by a wealthy person who allocated a certain amount of money for the teaching of young children by a monk or priest. In return, the students were directed by the priest to sing lengthy masses in the name of the school's founder, who hoped to achieve grace and immortality for his charity. The funds were usually placed in the chantry's treasury, which was under the direct control of appointed *feoffees* (trustees). These feoffees became responsible for the administration of the school, while the priest attended to the teaching duties.

The Jesuit Humanistic schools were particularly well organized and developed an early division of labor between *teachers* and *administrators* The *rector* was the chief administrator and the *prefect* was his assistant.

Many private schools and colleges have been controlled by boards of *trustees*. Privately operated schools in England (where they are called *public schools*) and America were and still are run by a *headmaster*. Once a teacher, the headmaster would typically be promoted to administrative rank much like that of the school *principal* in publicly operated modern schools. The headmaster was assisted by *ushers*, who performed the same duties as the modern-day assistant principal. Since public schools mushroomed in the 19th century, particularly in the United States, a more complex system of administration and supervision has developed. Probably the most significant factor involved in the development of a separate administrative profession has been the growth in size of the educational enterprise. Nowhere has this been more evident than in the United States.

The city schools were the first to become large enough to have so many teachers that a separate administration was required. The *principal*, or head teacher, was the first to act in an administrative capacity. Because of the unique American system of joint local and state control over education, the principal of the early 19th century was duty-bound to both. Most immediately, though, the principal was—and still is for the most part—particularly answerable to the local *school board*. Made up of elected or appointed local officials, the board was charged with supervising the schools and operating them in the most efficient manner available. The principal, and later the *assistant principal*, was appointed to handle these matters directly.

In the late 19th century, however, both state and municipal authorities began to encroach on the authority of the principal. New York State had been the first to organize state administrative agencies. As early as 1784 it had created a *State Board of Regents* and in 1812 the office of *state superintendent*. State boards of education were not very popular at that time, especially when New York's first superintendent, Gideon Hawley, irked the state legislature to the point that his office was dissolved until 1854. Greater success followed in Massachusetts and Connecticut, under Horace Mann and Henry Barnard, respectively. They proved that state superintendents could provide inspirational and effective guidance to the local and district management of public schools. This guidance was especially meaningful in light of the fact that both Mann and Barnard insisted that their administration of the schools could be only as effective as public participation allowed. They insisted on local involvement at the expense of strong state control. By the beginning of the 20th century, both state and city boards of education and superintendents were sharing significantly in the administration of schools.

School supervision was first recognized as an important ingredient of education in Prussia, where Johann Pestalozzi and Johann Herbart had a profound impact on the 19th-century normal school movement. Supervisors were regarded as teachers of teachers. They entered classrooms, held teachers' meetings, set up teacher institutes, and encouraged reading circles. They were, in effect, responsible for the in-service training, assistance, and encouragement of the teacher. This role has become increasingly important for the contemporary school administrator, such as the principal, who is often encouraged to delegate administrative duties to others, leaving more time for the training of teachers, assistant teachers, and auxiliary staff members.

During the 20th century the most significant development in the occupation of school administrator and supervisor has been in the area of professional training and preparation. This has been notable in the United States, where universal public education has warranted it most. The first two decades of the century saw the beginnings of professional curricula designed specifically for the prospective administrator. George D. Strayer of Teachers College, Columbia University, and Ellwood P. Cubberley

*Many school administrators started their formal days overseeing an assembly of students, here doing calisthenic exercises. (From* Frank Leslie's Popular Monthly Magazine, *September 17, 1881)*

of Stanford University were pioneers in this movement. Administrators were taught first of all to work cooperatively with one another and with other school personnel. Toward the close of the 19th century, many a court battle was fought over the respective power and authority of school boards, school officials, state superintendents, and various supervisors.

Throughout the world administrators in the 20th century have become increasingly involved in the issue of the economic efficiency of schools. In Britain, Sir Michael Sadler was one of the leaders in the survey movement, which has led administrators to take much closer looks at the cost efficiency and proper management of public schools. Surveys include reviews of building facilities, textbooks, janitorial services, student progress, and teacher certification. In short, they are a total examination of the use and efficiency of the school systems. While these surveys have been helpful in the more efficient management of schools and have even increased the levels of student progress in many cases, they are not without their drawbacks.

In America, educational surveys have become the chief governing tool of administrators and supervisors on all levels of public schooling. The aim has been for administrators to standardize the learning environment to attain the best possible results at the least public cost. Not only are financial matters and budgetary items under constant inspection but students, too, face an endless barrage of state, local, and national testing, designed to gauge a district's effectiveness. However, such standardized tests are poor indicators of such educational factors as creativity, perception, and adaptability. They are strictly attuned to measure the development of preconceived skills and the learning of desired information. Some American college administrators have dropped requirements that student applications include standardized entrance examination scores. Reasons cited for this include the inability of such tests to properly gauge intellectual or professional potential and the tests' disregard of cultural diversity, which tends to place ethnic minorities at a disadvantage.

Unfortunately, many public school administrators still rely heavily on standardized tests. Even kindergarten students are now being tested and categorized. Surveys of this nature (and even those relating to the competency of teachers, the management of buildings and grounds, and the effectiveness of curricular and program design) are certainly convenient and neat. They allow administrators to classify students for the sake of comparative analyses. They may also be used to demonstrate the effectiveness of a school program to the community when it is time for the annual budget to be approved, and to state inspectors when financial aid is sought. But such statistics are also very often misleading indicators of effectiveness, because many other valuable results are far more difficult to measure.

The profession of educational administrator and supervisor is a difficult and often thankless one. Administrators are responsible for institutions that are supposed to be run as financially responsible businesses, on the one hand, and community service organizations, on the other. They are held accountable for the progress of students, the reliability and competency of teachers, and the proper use and maintenance of facilities. With universal education an increasingly present reality in the world, they have a large burden indeed. As they attempt to ease it with reliance on objective financial surveys and standardized testing, they stand to be blamed for a narrow perception of educational ideals. If they attach themselves to the highest regard for sound educational idealism and dedicate themselves exclusively to the intellectual and emotional maturity of the students whom the institutions supposedly serve, they are often blamed for fiscal liberalism, poor business management, and the failure of students to live up to community, parental, and bureaucratic expectations. On the other hand, administrators enjoy high social status and can consider themselves to be at the apex of their profession.

For related occupations in this volume, *Scholars and Priests*, see the following:

Monks and Nuns
Priests
Scholars
Teachers

# Teachers

Teaching goes back to the beginning of civilization. As humans began to accumulate knowledge about the world and themselves, they developed means to pass it on to others. In most early societies—as in many non-literate or isolated parts of the world even into modern times—this teaching was done quite informally, within the family or clan. Education was often centered on the local religious leader, who passed on both beliefs and knowledge. That would be the pattern for much of history.

Teaching as a profession really began when humans developed the practice of recording information by writing. *Teachers* were then employed to instruct others in these techniques and later in the finer points of composition and specialized research.

## The Near East

In ancient Egypt and Mesopotamia (modern Iraq), the first schools were in the temples and palaces. Priestly *scribes* taught students the basics of writing. Most of the instruction was oral and had to be memorized. Usually skilled scribes working for a fee, these teachers were frequently housed and fed in the temple, palace, or pyramid complex. Their schools were often only rooms within a larger institution, such as a temple, rather than separate schoolhouses. Teachers taught long hours and were quick to use physical punishment on slow, lazy, or sloppy students. Some scribal teachers worked in writing rooms called "tablet houses" only on a part-time basis, working the rest of the time at record keeping, mathematical computation, and correspondence. Some enterprising teachers opened private schools for would-be scribes in their own homes.

Like other literate professionals, teachers of early Egypt and Mesopotamia were almost always recruited from among the elite upper classes, for only those of high economic standing could afford to send their sons to scribal schools. The occupation had some notable benefits. Teachers were part of a revered elite made powerful by working with words. Many teachers compiled personal

*Early or modern, teachers have always, it seems, been annoyed when a pupil is late. (Rheinisches Landesmuseum, Trier, Roman, c. second century A.D.)*

libraries (small by modern standards) from the copying assignments they gave their students. Others received extra earnings from tutoring students privately outside of the regular classroom setting. Teachers were important because their assessments of a student's capabilities not only determined whether or not he could graduate to a higher level of learning, but often dictated the degree of success or failure that a graduate would find in his chosen career. So crucial were teachers' evaluations that numerous stories survive of parents bribing them with praise, feasts, and riches to get more favorable appraisals for their children.

## The East

Similar situations existed farther east in ancient times. China's system of village schools and regional colleges dates back to at least a thousand years B.C. Even then educational achievement was used as a basis for selection into the civil service. Instructors stressed thorough learning of the basic language and notation systems, using bamboo books. Beyond this they gave their students a complete indoctrination into the manners, ethics, and social codes of conduct expected of the educated person, relying as much on example as on oral instruction. Simple rote learning was condemned, on the basis that—as Confucius would later say—"learning without thought is labor lost." Village schoolmasters provided education to the poor as well as the rich, even to men and women after a day's work in the fields.

The fifth century B.C. was a time of political decentralization and the school systems disintegrated somewhat as a result. But this was, surprisingly, a great age for education and for literacy in general. Rival states within China vied in attracting the best scholars to their courts; once under royal patronage, these scholars established private schools, passing on their philosophies to interested students. This was the Age of the Hundred Schools.

Unfortunately it was followed by a repressive, book-burning period, in which the private schools suffered as once the public institutions had done—and in which many teachers were condemned to death for refusing to give up their books. With the establishment of the Han Dynasty in the third century B.C., education was again revived. The once-banned books of Confucius were made the centerpiece of an educational system that would, up into modern times, be focused on preparing the best students for entrance examinations for the highly respected, very desirable government service.

Education in early India was also closely tied to the political needs of society. Hindu India was sharply stratified into a caste system, based on heredity and tied to professional distinctions. Teachers were Brahmins, members of the highest, priestly caste. As such, they were the chief interpreters of the sacred Hindu writings called the *Vedas*. These teachers established forest schools (*asramas*) in rural areas. After some years of home teaching, students went to live at a forest school as part of their teacher's family. No fees were paid. Students received room, board, and an education—the curriculum varying with their caste. The teacher, in turn, obtained the students' free labor for house and farm work, such as minding the cattle, during the years of schooling. Teachers stressed memorization, though always emphasizing understanding as well. They especially stressed memorization of the *Vedas* and attempted to instill the social and ethical values these writings contained.

## The Greeks

The education of the early Greeks also stressed the political and social interests of society. Following the example set by the Athenians, the Greeks generally thought education should be aimed at training young men in the art of citizenship. As such, education eventually came to be viewed as a service undertaken by and for the state. Females were banned from taking part in formalized learning. However, most free male citizens between the ages of six and fourteen were eligible to be students if their parents could pay the tuition.

Formal schools appeared in Athens sometime after the seventh century B.C. By the fifth century B.C., during the Classical Age, they were flourishing. Because of the cosmopolitan character of Athenian life and the sophisticated political structure of the city-state, education was quite varied as well as widespread. Although privately operated, the tuition-paid schools were closely monitored and rather strictly regulated by the state, especially regarding the curriculum. Physical education was considered an essential part of the development of citizens who were to be capable of defending their state, so the building and maintenance of gymnasiums for students was publicly funded.

At the highest level of teaching were the great philosophers of the day—some of whom were more famous as *scholars* than simply as teachers. *Sophists* were the largest group of teachers. They traveled from city to city delivering their insights and thoughts to paying students, who eagerly sought the wisdom for which they were famous throughout the Hellenistic world. They taught primarily through lecture. Some attending students took notes, but most depended on their abilities to memorize the greater and most significant portions of the content so presented. The Greeks were keenly adept at this practice—so much so that they frequently disdained the use of writing and reading as tools of higher intellectual pursuit.

Together, the scholarly Sophists made up a sort of informal university, representing the greatest and most prominent intellectual ideas of their times. They were not without critics, however. Many people believed that it was immoral to accept money for sharing ideas that would benefit the state. The great philosopher Socrates shared this view. He persistently refused pay for the wisdom and insight that he readily shared, believing that such compensation represented a conflict of interest. He felt that teachers should feel free to condemn society—as he himself frequently did—but would not do so if that very society provided their living.

Besides the issue of payment, the Sophists were attacked for demoralizing the citizenry, rather than uplifting it. Many Sophists taught that the individual and his beliefs were more important than the state and its needs and rules. Such teaching was often thought to border on subversion, and several of these wandering men of knowledge were jailed, exiled, deported, or condemned to death, as Socrates was.

The Greeks were the first people to foster education on a grand scale. They did so for political reasons more than for intellectual achievement, which they held was useless unless practically applied to the improvement of the state. The Sophists, many thought, were too inclined to underscore the rights of the individual and the fantasies of the intellect at the expense of the development of a responsible (and obedient) citizenry and techniques for improving the efficiency and strength of the state.

The lower levels of teaching—corresponding roughly to what we would now call elementary and secondary education—received less attention and stirred less controversy, but they also were given less acclaim and esteem. Essentially three types of teachers were engaged in the formal instruction of young men: the music teacher (*citharist*), the athletic teacher of the gymnasium (*paedotribe*), and the teacher of letters (*grammatist*).

In the later days of the Golden Age, the *grammatists* came to be the most respected members of the elementary teaching profession. This was the time of the great Greek literature, philosophy, and drama. The Sophists emphasized the importance of rhetoric—skill at public speaking and persuasive argument—and intellectual reasoning in the proper development of the individual. It was a time when letters and ideas came to outweigh good citizenship, military training, and physical skill.

Although the *grammatist* began to dominate the teaching profession in terms of prestige and following, attracting much more business than his counterparts, he, too, was not above reproach. Many men recalled the days of glory and valor when the young men had brought home war victories and Olympic prizes. They blamed the new emphases on individualism and intellectualism for the loss of piety in religion, the lack of training in military skills, and the rise of professional *athletes*, corrupting the old amateur traditions.

Ultimately the status of teachers was an individual matter. Those who had the best reputations for getting their students to learn desired skills and ideas were the ones who gathered the most students and could charge the highest tuitions. It was often a matter of prestige to say that one's son studied with a certain teacher, as people today might boast that their children graduated from Harvard. Education was fully teacher-oriented. There were really no schoolhouses—indeed, much of the instruction was given in open air facilities. The *grammatist*, *citharist*, and *paedotribe* taught letters, music, and athletics respectively in their own separate establishments. A student would spend certain hours of the long school day at each of their meeting places. Occasionally the teachers of letters and music would combine facilities to make their establishment more convenient and therefore more attractive to students.

Although Greek education was a far more formal system of instruction than had been know elsewhere in the ancient world, it was quite informal by today's standards. Teachers were not obliged to undergo any specific periods or types of training in preparation for their careers. Most of them had received the elementary education that they set out to teach, but no strict guidelines were set. Many a teacher with poor qualifications attracted students to his establishment sheerly on the basis of his personal appeal. Others charged fees low enough to bring in children whose parents could not afford more reputable instructors. Many parents also employed *pedagogues*, who were men assigned to watch over a young boy's education, for example, to see that he got to his classes and prepared his assignments. Some teachers and many pedagogues were actually *slaves*, generally prisoners captured in war. Many slaves were extremely well educated themselves and were more than qualified to teach. Other philosophers needed no more qualifications to practice their self-ordained profession than did elementary teachers. In fact, many complained of colleagues who were little more than persuasive rhetoricians, that is, men skilled in public speaking and logical argument.

In Greece, education was not an end in itself. Teachers commanded the respect and gratitude of parents, students, and society to the extent that they delivered tools, techniques, and information that could be applied to a craft, a business, or the duties of citizenship. Teachers tried hard to win that respect and gratitude, to attract not only students but also endowments and sometimes even public employment. Many of the more reputable teachers were given grants by wealthy citizens, aristocrats, and even kings so that they could carry on their good work. Others were employed by cities throughout the Hellenistic world, becoming in a sense public officials. They were paid salaries and even pensions out of public funds. Some such instructors obtained their positions through invitation but—surprisingly—even more of them did so through general elections.

As far as educational progress was concerned, teachers were evaluated by society in terms of the practicality and social expediency of their instruction. Teachers could not hide behind their own evaluations of students in order to justify their effectiveness. Grades, examinations, and reports played a very insignificant role in education, particularly in the higher forms such as the lectures by the Sophists. If students did not learn what was pertinent and practical—or even worse, if they learned what was *im*pertinent and *im*practical—the teacher was held to account.

### The Romans

In the ancient Roman civilization, the family provided the basis of education. It was not until the end of the second century B.C. that formal schools became common, and this was due mostly to the influence of Greek culture. The main sources of formal education by that time were the elementary schools known as the *ludi*. These were run by the *ludi magister*, or *litterator*, who was especially adept in the languages and arts. Reading, writing, and arithmetic dominated the curriculum of the *ludi*. Latin translations of Homer's *Odyssey* usually served as the basis of instruction. Physical training and music found little place in such programs. Indeed, the Romans frequently pointed to them as examples of what they believed to be the impracticality and feminine nature of Greek education. The *ludus* was a private school with little government sanction, aid, restriction, regulation, or even interest. It was open to both boys and girls between the ages of seven and twelve. The *litterator* received most of his business from wealthy upper-class parents. In addition, parents typically assigned to each child a *pedagogue*. As in Greece, the pedagogue was a close companion and guardian of the school child. Many pedagogues were well-educated and capable Greek slaves, so they often acted also as private tutors. (Many such slaves were prisoners of war taken by the Romans.) *Litterators* occasionally complained that these slaves could not offer the quality of education that the *litterators* could. Such arguments were invariably based on the supposed impracticality and softness of Greek education, of which many a pedagogue was a product.

The secondary school was run by a *grammaticus*, who—like his Greek models—emphasized intellectual above physical or artistic achievement. His students were boys between the ages of 12 and 16. Initially, he taught only Greek. Latin was later included and gradually became the main language of study. Generally a teacher chose one language or the other for all instruction, so that for many years Latin grammar schools were separate from Greek ones. Latin grammar schools were found in every province and every town in the Roman Empire during its greatest days of glory. The *grammaticus*, like the *ludi magister*, ran a private school in his own home or privately arranged facility. Catering mostly to wealthy students, he charged a rather high fee for tuition and operated essentially free from government controls.

During the period of the Roman Empire, the rhetorical school was widely established as the generally accepted institution of higher learning. *Rhetoricians*—mostly from Greece, or with strong backgrounds in Greek oratory—attracted throngs of upper-class children, especially those from the senatorial faction of society. They taught practical styles of public speaking designed specifically to further the careers of aspiring *statesmen*. The rhetorician, even more than other teachers in Rome, served a very narrow and privileged class. Because public speaking was then held in great esteem, rhetoricians received widespread fame. By the final days of the Republic, Julius Caesar had granted many foreign rhetoricians voting and citizenship rights if they would establish schools in Rome. A similar class of teachers in the Eastern Roman Empire taught Greek rhetoric. It was those in the West, teaching in Latin, who were most highly esteemed. After all, who could better manipulate public opinion than the great statesmen who, like Cicero, were so well versed in the mechanics and persuasive styles of rhetoric?

*Litterators* were not held in high regard. Like the *pedagogues*, many *litterators* were Greek slaves, and so had no social position. They needed few credentials to "open up shop." Teaching reading to small children was not considered a very adventurous, or ambitious, masculine calling in the days when great Roman armies were overpowering the Mediterranean world.

Grammarians and rhetoricians, however, enjoyed much greater esteem in the Roman world, whether they were of Roman or Greek birth. In fact, for some time Greeks were rather preferred to Romans, since they were believed to have had much more thorough training in the profession of teaching. Higher level teaching posts did not demand any great evidence of scholarship. Men were deemed sufficiently prepared to assume the duties of the occupation once they had studied for a fair amount of time with one of the recognized masters; those who had done do were highly sought.

The teachers of ancient Rome did not organize as a professional class, apart from belonging to their specific rhetorical or philosophical schools. They needed no formal qualifications to engage in their occupations. They needed only to provide evidence of study with a reputable teacher, and to show a general familiarity with the liberal arts. Credentials were deemed relatively insignificant for elementary school teachers, who taught only the basic principles of reading, writing, and calculation. The grammarians developed a broader curriculum that included history, ethics, poetry, grammar, and literary criticism. The rhetoricians, likewise, began to offer a broad course that enabled the student to become, in the words of Quintilian, *"vir bonus dicendi peritus"*—the virtuous man skilled in speaking.

In the Early Empire grammarians and rhetoricians were thought to be extremely important, responsible for teaching students morality and ethics combined with a liberal literary education. The ideal was to have students develop and use all of their intellectual skills in the service of the state. In the Later Empire, however, these ideals vanished. Teachers living comfortably on public support were strongly encouraged to avoid controversial and impractical subjects and philosophies. Their instruction became sterile and narrow, and they increased their already overzealous use of physical punishment and abuse as teaching techniques. Grammarians restricted their instruction to routine studies of phonetics, verb conjugations, and noun declensions, focusing on memorizing and repeating. Rhetoricians became obsessed with oratory skills in and of themselves—devoid of any interpretation and understanding of the political or philosophical context within which statesmen or even citizens lived and worked.

There was, by this time, another class of teachers—the Christians. They had been variously persecuted, tolerated, and finally accepted by the state. Although Constantine had earlier invited these teachers to enter the professional ranks, Julian decreed in 362 that they could not work in the publicly supported schools, to which only the emperor could confirm appointments. But by the sixth century, Justinian was closing the schools of Athens because he declared their earlier instruction to be pagan. Clearly, during the closing centuries of the empire, Christian teaching had come to be accepted not only in its own right but as a form of instruction superior to that available at the secular schools.

The religious teachers were usually *priests* or *monks*. Their teaching was hardly more creative than that of their secular counterparts. They showed little interest in liberal arts, or in intellectual or aesthetic development, except as these subjects had direct bearing on religious life and church doctrine. But after the barbarians sacked Rome and almost destroyed Western civilization for centuries to come, it was the priests and monks who kept a vestige of the teaching profession alive. Working steadfastly behind the protective stone walls of monasteries, they preserved and copied, learned and taught, not only the great work of Christian authors and theologians but even some of the least offensive pagan and secular literature.

## Changes in the East

The tradition of secular education—and many writings of the Greco-Roman world—did survive farther east, in Persia, brought there by Nestorian Christians fleeing a charge of heresy. Especially under the Sassanids in the third to seventh centuries, Persian teachers worked not only in court schools, teaching upper-class children, but also in institutions of higher education, most notably the academy of Gundishapur. Teaching both the arts and sciences, these schools drew on both the Western traditions and those of India.

In India itself, the forest schools were no longer. By the fifth century B.C., Brahmins had begun moving into the cities, no longer restricting themselves to religious or educational callings. Brahmin teachers began establishing schools in towns and villages throughout the land, teaching students, including adults, without regard to caste. Experts in various fields, such as medicine, law, and soldiering, also banded together to form academies for professional education in several cities. In this period, Buddhists set up monastic schools, primarily for those studying for the priesthood. After the third century B.C., with the rapid spread of Buddhism, these monastic schools increasingly offered secular education as well. Higher education also flourished in India in succeeding centuries. When the Roman Empire was declining in the West, the University of Nalanda alone had over 1,500 teachers.

Farther east, the T'ang dynasty was bringing a golden age to China in the seventh through tenth centuries. Many teachers found employment in the schools that were maintained in towns, villages, and districts. These schools, some under local control and some under the central government, provided basic education. Beyond that level were other, more advanced schools, generally established in cities. Some of these focused on specific subjects, such as medicine or law. Others were less formal schools, groups of students that gathered around noted scholars. Many of them were Buddhists or Taoists, for in T'ang times diversity of religious belief was warmly tolerated.

Other schools, often attached to the imperial court, were geared toward placing the most capable men in civil service positions. Teachers who taught young men—mostly aristocrats—the skills necessary for state employment were usually *scribes* and *soldiers*, who taught literature, calligraphy, and the martial arts. One of their most important social functions was to teach students in the ways and manners of Chinese culture, especially giving them an understanding of Confucianism. Chinese court instructors were deemed extremely important in maintaining the economic, political, and social status quo. As a result they were carefully controlled by the emperor, as was the curriculum they developed.

Many teachers in China's court schools were men who had themselves failed to obtain official positions in the government. It is ironic that those who did poorly in civil service examinations made careers out of instructing others to do better. These teachers enjoyed social esteem and recognition, and were more than amply rewarded for their work. But it is no surprise that their overall social status was lower than that of public officials—those who scored well enough on their examinations to be placed in state service positions.

While Chinese teachers were flourishing under the T'ang dynasty, Islam was rising in western Asia. Drawing on the Classical traditions that had been preserved in Persia, the Moslem culture soon developed a diverse and widespread educational system. Almost every town had its elementary writing schools, and almost every mosque had a school to teach people to read the Koran. By the 10th century in Baghdad there were an estimated 3,000 mosques, most with schools. Even the peoples on the fringe of Islam, notably in sub-Saharan Africa, had "bush schools" for the same purpose, taught by local religious leaders. Upper-class students, and those intended for higher education or office, often attended court schools after receiving their elementary education.

In a time when learning was honored, many other people also became teachers. Individual scholars often established *circle schools*, so-called because the scholar would sit in the middle of the group, sometimes slightly raised, with visiting scholars and the most advanced students forming circles around him, with the less advanced students making up the outer circles. Wherever books were sold or collected—at bookshops or scribes' libraries—similar informal schools would result from the gathering of interested pupils, often with one person acting as mentor, or leader.

These schools were, however, highly variable in the content and quality of education offered. As a result, the Islamic leaders established a system of public schools, in which the curriculum was more defined, the physical facilities better suited to education, and the teachers

*Small Moslem schools like this one taught students how to read, primarily so they could read the* Koran. *(From* History of India, *by Fannie Roper Feudge, 1903)*

trained and supervised according to more general standards. They were better paid in the bargain. This type of school system spread eastward to India, where Buddhist and Hindu schools were in decline, and westward to Spain, where it later helped spark Europe's Renaissance.

## Medieval Europe

In the Western world, the Christian clerics—priests, monks, and nuns—carried on the functions of teaching throughout the medieval centuries, before the dawning of the Renaissance brought new interest in secular learning. In Europe, the Catholic Church generally operated religious schools, designed to teach people how to carry out their responsibilities as Christians. Since the written language was primarily Latin, the masses of people could not comprehend even religious services without the additional training that was provided by the church schools. However, such an education was hardly liberal and usually avoided (or roundly condemned) secular topics and issues, except as they bore on church doctrine. The teachers of these schools were dogmatic and provincial in their training, outlook, and instruction. They were not professional but undertook the job of educating the young as an additional church-related duty.

Charlemagne was one of Europe's few patrons of learning during this period of history. The sorry status of the teaching profession during even his enlightened reign (768-814) is reflected by some of his decrees. For one, he had to plead with (and eventually demand that) the cleric-teachers first learn to read and write properly themselves before trying to teach others about religious doctrines or anything else. Additionally, he demanded that the church develop free schools throughout the land to instruct children in the rudiments of reading and writing.

Since the church controlled most education, there was little vocational or secular instruction. However, there were always some modest public and private schools operating in medieval towns, especially in Italy. Some teachers were paid by public support systems, while others charged a fee for group instruction and private tutoring. Like the Roman teachers before them, they tended to emphasize grammar and rhetoric.

Nonpublic secular education was stimulated in the later Middle Ages by the rise of trade and the accompanying growth of professional occupations. The result was what we might call *vocational education*, except that it was much more practical and informal than such education tends to be today. Even in the early Middle Ages a sort of vocational training was available to those wishing to learn a craft. But there were no trained teachers involved and no specific techniques of instruction. Most of the learning was a matter of a young child imitating a parent or another worker, in this way learning how to go about making something or providing a desired service. As towns and trade guilds developed after the 11th century, more formalized techniques and systems of instructing vocational apprentices evolved.

The common method of schooling that emerged was that of binding a young boy to a *master craftsman*, who agreed to teach him the essential skills and knowledge of a particular trade, as well as the rudiments of reading and writing. The master was also obliged by the contractual agreement (*indenture*) to oversee the boy's moral and religious growth. The "student," in return, agreed to work steadfastly for the master and never to divulge to outsiders the nature or mechanics of the skills involved in the trade. In this manner, guilds were able to demand the highest prices for their works and services, while at the same time severely limiting the amount and quality of potential competition. The master, or teacher, involved in this system was trained almost exclusively in the art of his vocation. This was the greater portion of the subsequent curriculum that he designed for his young pupil. As a result, this system led to a rift between intellectual and vocational forms of education and classifications of teachers. The master was first a craftsman and only incidentally a professional instructor.

Another medieval form of secular education that made use of teachers and instructors was the chivalrous education of the *knight*. Arranged somewhat systematically by the overlord, classes were conducted at the lord's court, although no special schools were created for this training. The instructors were from various backgrounds—*priests, knights, minstrels*, and others. It is not altogether clear whether they specialized in teaching or not. Most probably, they were generally wealthy and respected leaders of society, who aided in the education of the rising generation of aristocrats out of loyalty to their lord and his court. Instruction was largely of a social nature, including the teaching of proper manners and etiquette, as well as dancing, singing, and conversation. Some intellectual learning was included in the overall program, but it was much less important than the social and military training that dominated the curriculum.

Until the 12th century the most meaningful intellectual education that existed was found in the monastery, cathedral, priory, and abbey. There at the lowest and most common levels priests in training were instructed on religious ceremony and duty; at the highest levels they were taught the whole range of subjects covered in these times. The teaching profession had become intertwined with church posts, especially with that of the chancellor of education (the *scholasticus*) of the leading monasteries of the age.

Many a *scholasticus* became so involved in his duties as teacher and scholar that he quite overlooked his more sacred calling. The scholasticus eventually obtained from the *bishops* the right and authority to choose the teaching staff at the cathedral school and, moreover, to issue a teaching license (*licentia docendi*) to the most highly qualified among them. Later, he was given the authority to grant teachers a license to teach outside of the licensing cathedral. This license (*licentia docendi ubique*) permitted teachers to travel to other cathedrals to present and share their ideas. In time, certain cathedrals gained considerable reputations, as their instructors journeyed about the land spreading the academic word. Students began to flock to the most prominent cathedrals, particularly those at Paris, Chartres, Bologna, Padua, and Salerno. The legendary British universities of Cambridge and Oxford were soon added to this list.

Teachers eventually sought professional protection from the forms of intellectual control often exercised by the church and its officers, specifically the bishop and the scholasticus. Toward this end, they formed an organized union, or professional guild, known as the universitas, or university. Academic freedom, then, was the motivation for the birth of the university, a place where teachers could openly instruct students without harassment. Students, too, had their own guilds within the system, to protect their rights against abuses from the teaching profession.

The universities—at first little more than conventions of faculty guilds—had a great influence on the development of the modern teaching profession. The university *professors* who acquired notable acclaim were really scholars, of a different class than the teachers of young school children. Their methods of instruction and organization were exemplary. Separate faculties of liberal arts, law, rhetoric, medicine, theology, and philosophy were combined in one institution. The professors, badgered as they were by both religious and state authorities, insisted on their right to uphold a certain standard of instruction that was not religious or political but *educational*.

For centuries education had been viewed as the means to ends designed by church, state, or both combined. In the hands of the trade guilds, it was a tool for the development and exclusivity of craftsmanship. As a guide to chivalrous attitudes and manners, it was a means for social control, cultivating a distinct and superior aristocracy to rule the vast peasantry that had no share in this education. But the university furthered the notion of education as being sufficient in its own right—a notion that had not been prominently held since the illustrious era of the ancient Greek philosophers.

Apart from being scholars, university professors influenced the modern development of the teaching profession in some concrete ways. In particular, they set standards for the organization of the profession. For example, the University of Paris was a corporation of masters from all over the city who had developed considerable student followings while teaching at the cathedral schools of Notre Dame, Ste. Genevieve, St. Victor, and others. They joined into a common guild to protect themselves from government and church restrictions.

As instructors, however, university professors were still bound by some rather strict conventions regarding their teachings. Students' views were very important, because tuition fees were the sole source of teachers' pay.

As the later Middle Ages drew to a close there was a gradual increase in the demand for elementary and secondary schoolteachers. Parish churches in the towns or on the manors made increased efforts to provide the rudiments of education to children, particularly those of the aristocracy. Teachers drawn from the priesthood taught part time in these *parish schools*. They also taught in the handful of *chantry* and *guild schools* that had been established. Both were early forms of private schools, which provided some foundation for the modern development of public education—and therefore of the secular teaching profession. Chantry schools were essentially schools that had been donated by wealthy individuals who sought favor with the church. The guild schools were supported by groups of wealthy persons who sought quality education for their children. Like the chantry, they, too, were placed under church control and priests taught the classes.

Instruction in the parish, grammar, guild, and chantry schools—which made up elementary and secondary education—was mostly oral. In the chantry, pupils chanted in unison phrases that had been dictated. In all types of schools, memorization of oral lessons was the basis of the learning experience. Recitation of long segments of lectures and lessons was demanded, since the teacher usually had the only textbook available. The days were long for student and teacher alike. And instructors were urged to spare no energy in severely punishing the pupil who would dare waste time by disregarding his lesson.

Teachers needed few credentials to obtain employment or appointment and were often poorly educated themselves. They did not have to demonstrate any teacher training in terms of instructional techniques, but only a crude familiarity with subject matter. After all, it was firmly held that students had only to learn the content of any given subject, and that was purely a matter of memorization. This process involved a professional "teacher" solely in a custodial capacity, to keep order, present factual information, promote appropriate social and moral behavior, and mete out necessary punishments. Teachers were not considered to play any part in whether or not a student actually learned or comprehended; that was strictly the student's business.

Throughout the day the schoolmaster was busy lecturing and punishing, commonly striking the errant student on the open palms with a paddle. He always spoke in Latin—the language of the Catholic Church—and pupils were obliged to do so as well. All knew that speaking one's native language—the vernacular—would be met with certain *vae natibus*, or "woe to the buttocks."

## Europe in the Renaissance

The Renaissance period drastically changed the focus and direction of education. There was a revival of interest in the classics written in Greek and especially Latin. At the same time there was growing commercial activity accompanied by a rising middle class of merchants, traders, and businessmen. Towns became political units, which strongly rivaled manors as the centers of the economy and popular culture. The overwhelming effect of these changes was the beginning of a secularization of education that would ultimately free most schools and teachers from the fetters imposed by the Catholic Church.

The rise of the middle class meant a broader population for teachers to serve. Many of the new students were

*The switch, as pointer or punisher, was long a teacher's basic tool. (Attributed to Albrecht Dürer, 1510)*

drawn from the families of merchants and business owners, who were barely educated themselves. These new schools were more likely to draw teachers from the university than from the priesthood. In addition, the schools focused on education as a practical preparation for town and business life, rather than as the refinement of manners that had dominated the schools of chivalry and many of the parish schools as well. The result was the development of humanistic secondary schools, which required more highly qualified and motivated professional teachers than had been known to the medieval world.

The humanist teachers developed curricula and methods of instruction based on the viewpoint—contrary to large segments of church dogma—that humans could control their own lives and destinies to a considerable extent. This was not to deny that God's grace and direction were necessary, but rather that such gifts could be enhanced by application of natural intelligence and powers of reason. Many humanists were greatly inspired by and indebted to the church doctrines of knowledge and education, while others assumed more skeptical postures on this issue. The common thread that bound them together was their concern for a thorough teaching of and reverent regard for grammar, rhetoric, and classical literature. The Catholic Church did not always approve of this emphasis. For one thing, classical literature was regarded as pagan and often in conflict with Christian values. Additionally, it did not stress the moral discipline that, for centuries, the parish schools had taught almost exclusively, along with themes of piety and atonement.

The humanist schools originated in Italy, but as the cultural and intellectual climate of the Renaissance spread to other parts of Europe, they became recognized as the *college* and *lycée* in France, the *gymnasium* in Germany, and the Latin grammar school in England and later in America. Although the teachers of these schools were supposedly faced with the task of rudimentary instruction, they were, in fact, obliged to teach on many different levels. Children who attended their schools varied in age from seven to twenty-one years old, so that the curriculum had to be one that progressed with the age and ability of the students. Reading, writing, and Latin syntax were taught early, but the works of classic authors were introduced as soon as possible. They formed the basis of learning from that point on. The study of Greek was reserved for older students.

Overall, the humanistic teacher was supposed to create an atmosphere and a curriculum within which a student could develop a well-rounded personality—strong of body and mind as well as spirit. The goal was to produce students who had a general knowledge and command of as many things as possible—reading, writing, fighting, painting, singing, medicine, and law. To attain such results, the instructor was supposed to avoid the popular method of physically punishing and pressuring the student into learning—or at least remembering—set material. Instead, he was to rely on social accountability and personal competition to spark the student's attention. Despite the unwritten humanist credo, the actual techniques of painting, dancing, and other arts were seldom taught by the humanistic teacher. Rather, he labored to instill an appreciation of artistic, cultural, esthetic, and even technical endeavors, so that the student was sufficiently inspired to pursue them on his own. The techniques themselves were considered a matter for the craft master, not the teacher. As a result, grammar and literature were the basis of the humanistic education.

Educational theory and educational practice are often far apart. So it was with humanistic schools. In theory, the teacher—more commonly called *master*—was supposed to be personally involved in the well-rounded physical, artistic, and intellectual education of the school's students. But teachers actually dwelled on grammar, rhetoric, and literature; they gave practically no attention to anything else. Although physical punishment and abuse were condemned by much of the humanistic literature, they actually formed the basis of classroom order.

The threat of punishment provided the primary motivation to endure boring lessons that were the constant task of the student. The Italian poet and scholar Petrarch once summarized the outstanding qualities that a teacher ought to possess in view of this situation:

> Let those . . . teach who like disorder, noise, and squalor; who rejoice in the screams of the victim as the rod falls gaily, who are not happy unless they can terrify, flog, and torture.

Masters, aided by assistants called *submasters*, typically began the day's work with a 7:00 A.M. flogging of students for the previous day's offenses. They were particularly strict in forbidding any pupil from speaking in the vernacular—the popular language of everyday life. Initiates—that is, those students new to the school—were not allowed to speak at all. Certainly this was far from the liberal, humane, general education called for by the most eloquent spokesmen of humanism.

Emerging quietly from the broad shadow cast by the humanistic schools were the vernacular schools, the sources of education for the common man. The rise of business, merchant, and craft guilds led to the development of large and densely populated towns and burghs. As the middle class developed in the towns of northern Europe and Italy, it demanded instruction that could meet its everyday needs of reading, writing, and computation. The rising middle class had little concern for abstract intellectual achievement or the impractical rigors of training the mind with the intense practice and memorization of declensions and grammatical rules involved in the bookman's language, Latin. The vernacular schools—being secular in origin, purpose, and control—were strongly opposed by Catholic Church authorities, if only because their rise to prominence meant the foreclosure of a significant portion of the church's centuries-old control over education.

Teachers at these vernacular schools were obliged to instruct pupils in the keeping of business accounts and the writing of letters and give them a familiarity with legal regulations affecting the family business. Invariably appointed and paid by municipal authorities, these teachers were salaried, though not very well. They were often the objects of scorn and ridicule, especially from the aristocracy and the humanists, who thought it hardly worthy to instruct children to use a language that they had long since already learned in the home and that was not even a part of church services. Still, the budding force of professional teachers of the vernacular had begun to make itself felt, even though it was confined strictly to the elementary schools. There was certainly little demand that such teaching go beyond the lower levels, since it existed only to fulfill the most practical and primary educational needs of the middle classes.

Many teachers during this era found employment as palace tutors. They taught in much the same manner as had been common in the schools of chivalry except with new emphasis on culture and literature, owing to humanistic influences. Some of the most eminent educational scholars of the day accepted positions as head schoolmasters at aristocratic courts. Vittorino da Feltre was invited to conduct school for the Duke of Mantua in the early 1400's. One of the most notable educators of the Renaissance, Vittorino took great pleasure in converting a splendid palace dwelling into a model humanistic school for children of both noble and lowly birth. He used a considerable portion of his earnings in housing and feeding those poor children. Palace teachers proved to be leading experimenters and practitioners in alternative curricular structures and instructional methods.

## The Protestant Reformation

The German schools of the Protestant Reformation period eventually began to open new doors for the teaching profession. This seems only fitting since the Reformation itself was born in Germany in the 16th century. There a new and powerful middle class had begun to clamor for a more equal social footing with the aristocracy—not least in the vernacular schools. This more democratic, common, and practical form of education had clear Protestant overtones. Many Reformation leaders equated education with the common person's right to know, learn, and interpret the Bible in their own vernacular, not to have the Bible's meaning handed down to people by church authorities.

The Protestant view clashed sharply with Catholic tradition. The result was long years of religious wars. These were as deeply rooted in the upheaval in old economic and political systems as in the theological disputes that were the obvious bones of contention. Adding confusion to the political and educational climate of the times was the increased distribution of printed books, pamphlets, and tracts. As the *printing press* revolutionized the art of gathering and dispensing information, it permitted many more people access to ideas that had previously been the exclusive domain of the aristocratic and ruling classes. For a broader reading public, works were translated and printed as vernacular books, which were widely distributed throughout all levels of society. As the middle classes—merchants, burghers, and the like—became better informed, they began to take a more active interest and role in both educational and religious institutions.

Perhaps the most critical issue affecting the history of this period, and certainly the underlying educational philosophy, was that concerning divine grace, destiny, good works, and how they contributed to salvation. For many centuries the Catholic Church had supported a corporate view of both Roman Catholicism and society. This meant simply that society was like a body, each part and limb having a distinct function as part of the whole. If one part of the body, or one member of society, failed to perform its duty, it was said, the whole body suffered a general illness that affected all the other parts. The same could be said of the Catholic Church, where the priesthood had certain functions, and lay people had others.

Education in the hands of the clergy was aimed at instructing children to know their social ranking and to do the best they could within it. Under no circumstances was the individual to try to break the divine order. The message was that one could honor God with good works but could not hope to improve his lot in life through active means. If God had intended for a person's lot to be better, the church preached, the person would have been born into a higher social class. Educators, being part of the church, had long supported this view of society. As such, it was a bulwark of the existing social, political, and economic order.

The new middle-class burghers of Germany felt differently. They had learned from mass-printed and widely distributed theological tracts written by Reformation thinkers that humans had the ability to interpret the Holy Scriptures for themselves. In so doing they would find out that people could and in fact should try to improve their lot in this life. For the Calvinists (and the later Puritans) salvation could come only through God's grace, but earthly success could be a sign of that salvation. This view encouraged people to be industrious, to show that they were among the saved—the "elect." Burghers, then, were able to line their pockets with capital and still be regarded as pious. Many Lutherans and other Protestants did not hold precisely the same view. But these notions formed the historical basis for what has since been called the *Protestant work ethnic*.

The teaching profession was profoundly altered by the ideas of the Protestant Reformation. The burgh schools were supported publicly, without the Catholic Church's involvement or approval. That made them secular in comparison with the parish and monastic schools. Moreover, their emphasis on practical arts and skills made them distinctly more secular.

Despite the considerable secular changes that took place in the vernacular elementary and secondary school curricula, teachers were still considered religious instructors, first and foremost. Vernacular schools in

Germany were the first schools of this type to be supported solely through state and municipal funding. In addition, they incorporated the relatively fresh notion of universal and compulsory education. As early as 1559 the Württemburg municipal authorities provided Protestant elementary schools and teachers for every village in the cosmopolitan area. Teachers were selected and salaried by the burgh to provide instruction in religion and church music primarily; reading and writing secondarily. Latin continued to play an important role, even in the vernacular schools, mainly because the largest body of available religious literature was written in it. The *Bible* was one of the chief textbooks that teachers relied on for social and moral instruction.

Germany was far ahead of its time in setting up public school systems, however.

In fact, the teaching profession was in grave turmoil with the advent of the Reformation. As the Catholic Church lost much of its prestige and influence, so did the parish schools and even the universities in many parts of Europe. But it was not a simple matter of vernacular and humanistic schools replacing them. Many people, especially of the middle class, lost confidence in education altogether. For one thing, they were convinced that it had become an impractical, overly intellectualized exercise in rhetoric and grammar. Charges were lodged that there had developed an overdependence and even obsession with the ideas of the Roman thinker Cicero, who stressed strict adherence to the rules of grammar and rhetoric. Called *Ciceronianism*, this approach to education was presumed to be based solely on the study of grammar for its own sake, not as it could be applied to reason or esthetics, to say nothing of the real world of business.

Another cause for the sudden drop in support for teachers and education during the early years of the Reformation was an economic situation created by the alterations in political and religious allegiances. With the Catholic Church suffering low public esteem and its schools losing both repute and tuition-paying enrollees, religious jobs of all sorts, and particularly those related to education, were becoming fewer and more competitive. Middle-class parents had previously made the investment of sending their children to parish schools largely so that they could use their learning as the basis for a religious career. Even aristocratic and noble families were strongly motivated to support such schools with an eye cast toward future official positions that their sons might obtain. So both middle-class and aristocratic parents had once had sufficient economic reason to send their sons through years of educational training, particularly at the numerous church-associated schools. Educated sons of aristocrats usually obtained official state appointments that were secular in nature. Sons of middle-class parents were placed in church positions that were less lucrative and prestigious but still secure and accompanied by a sufficiently respectable standing in the community.

With the decline in the Roman Catholic Church, however, a general economic upheaval ensued, in which both religious and secular offices were more difficult to obtain through educational training. To depress the already sad situation even further, many former patrons of parish schools withdrew their grants, which had gone far in supporting their operation, including the hiring of teachers. This was partly due to the Catholic Church's devalued image but also to the Reformation idea that good works (such as patronizing a school) were not sufficient for salvation.

The middle class also came to believe that, in the hands of the Catholic Church, education had been employed as a tool for social control. For many Europeans this view led to a distrust of priestly and religious teachers—which easily became a distrust for all teachers, even lay ones. Such caution was only enhanced by the fact that even the teachers of the vernacular and Protestant schools emphasized the Bible and Christian morality in their instruction. Of course, some Reformation leaders saw this instruction as progressive and liberating, aimed at supporting the development of the individual. But to many people, all teachers had become symbols of the status quo, reactionism, and even repression.

Martin Luther had been the leading force in the Protestant reform movement that so undermined established education. Much of the criticism registered against the schooling of the day was based on his insistence that hard work, diligence, and dogged industriousness were preferable to good works and idle piety. As theology and educational theory, this idea was especially appealing to the burghers and merchants of the main towns in Germany and other parts of northern Europe. They saw in Luther's teachings the basis for an educational upheaval. No longer would they let their sons be the tools of what they saw as social reactionism; no longer would they pay tuition to have them sitting all day in idleness, thinking of nothing more practical than ancient poetry and Christian morals—morals they believed were taught at home anyway. They believed education should be aimed squarely at the goals of vocation; all else was frivolity and Catholic.

Luther was astounded by this turn of events. He had never intended to apply the brakes to education, only to make it more pertinent to the lives of all people, and to insure that its constant goal was the fostering of Christian life and devotion. He saw education as one of the greatest undertakings of society—one that would make for better citizens and therefore better societies, and one that would enable the greater portion of the population to devote itself to the steadfast study of the Scriptures. He had proposed reforms in education but had instead succeeded in firing a revolution—in much the same way that his ideas for political reforms went beyond his control, until he eventually had to reject the very peasantry that had lionized him as a champion of the people.

Teaching, which Luther considered to be among the noblest of all callings, became a profession that was despised and considered repulsive. Elementary and secondary schools could find few students, and universities ran into similarly hard times. Appalled, Luther pleaded with common people and authorities to turn their attentions away from the struggle to survive in the world of work. Unable to convince parents to voluntarily send their children to school, he told civil authorities that they had better make education compulsory, before civility had vanished irretrievably.

Luther became a champion for the teaching profession. He understood that "parents see that they can no longer place their children upon the bounty of monasteries and cathedrals" and that they could no longer expect their children "to become priests, monks, and nuns, and thus to earn a support." The solution to this dilemma, he resolved, was not in abandoning education altogether. After all, how else could children learn to read, study, and understand the Bible for themselves, thus freeing themselves from the type of manipulation that the Catholic Church had been able to practice for so many years? Education, he preached, ought to be universal, so that all classes might attain the knowledge that God had provided freely in the Scriptures. Moreover, it ought to be compulsory, since people apparently did not know what was best for them and were likely to lose themselves totally in their minute concerns for the immediate world. Even at that, he thought school need only take up a few daily hours. The rest of the time, he conceded, might well be spent in vocational apprenticeship.

Luther deemed education to be the root of the good society. The notion that schooling benefited society at large placed the responsibility for sponsoring and sustaining it squarely on the civil authorities, who were supposedly concerned with social betterment. The ideas that Luther put into motion were to guide the progress of education and the growth of the teaching profession into new, previously unexplored areas up to the present day. Universal and compulsory schooling for all children between specified ages; practical and vocational implementation of ideas and methodologies; public creation and support of schools for all children as a social obligation—all of these notions are part and parcel of contemporary education. They formed a philosophical transition from medieval to modern times in the development of schools and the growth of the teaching profession. Yet the extent to which teachers today rely on the secular curriculum would not have pleased Luther at all. In his *Address to the Nobility* in 1520 he made clear his understanding of the deepest meaning of education: "Where the Holy Scriptures are not the rule," he declared, "I advise no one to send his child. Everything must perish where God's Word is not studied unceasingly."

## Early Modern Times

In the 16th and 17th centuries attempts were made to develop a better prepared and more highly qualified class of teachers than was available. Protestants and Catholics alike undertook teacher-training programs. Teachers were no longer thought of largely as custodians. People began to understand that teachers, by their curricula and methods, were actually shaping the minds and outlooks of students. This was especially true as new ideas, especially in science, began to reshape people's view of the world. As the modern era approached, teaching was bound to rival the pulpit itself in political, social, and economic influence.

The new interest in the teacher's influence, however, still focused on religious leadership. If the number and reputation of teachers were at their lowest level in years, steps had to be taken to improve their quality and therefore their status. Luther had long called for a well-trained and superbly disciplined core of teachers that would command the respect of pupils and their parents. In this way, the true word of God could be passed on convincingly and in an informed manner.

The Catholics, though, were the main innovators of teacher preparation. Based on their long experience in the field, the Jesuits prepared a major work for teacher training called the *Ratio Studorium*. The Jesuits were noted for turning out superbly qualified and knowledgable instructors. St. Jean Baptiste de La Salle had decided that the education of young children was extremely significant, coming as it did during the child's intellectually formative years. Determined to make elementary teaching an art and respectable profession, he thought of new ways of standardizing elementary instruction to make the job more manageable and efficient. He initiated the method of teaching students in graded classes, rather than individually, as had been the common practice.

The social and economic status of teachers slowly began to improve as they became better recognized as important, qualified, and specially trained professionals. In Germany, they were still paid largely through the tuition fees of pupils, but greater and more regular supplementary funds were forthcoming from both state and church treasuries. In some states, they were provided with social security, pension, and sickness aid. The German state of Saxe-Gotha in 1642 even volunteered salary increases for the teachers working in their school system.

Teaching was still deemed largely a religious calling, however. The Catholic Church had begun training teachers from the ranks of lay people who had no desire to be priests. Though most Protestant teachers were ministers, Protestants also used some lay people for academic instruction in their classrooms. Regardless of whether the teacher had a clerical or secular background, they taught the "three R's" as well as more technical and vocational subjects; they also taught literature in the vernacular, as well as in Latin, Greek, and even Hebrew. But the thrust of all their instruction was supposed to be essentially religious, based intimately on Christian ethics and morality.

Teacher supervision grew directly out of the desire of church and municipal authorities to monitor the religious appropriateness of the instruction that was being delivered in the schools. The very act of supervision attested to the growing recognition of the enormous influence that the teaching profession brought to bear on the younger generation and future leaders of society. The Calvinists were particularly watchful of teachers to insure that religious orthodoxy remained present in the instruction that was carried on in their schools. Still more careful in carrying out this function were the Puritans of England and especially North America, where their influence was the strongest.

The Catholics, too, began to pay closer attention to the teachers they employed to carry on the doctrines of what was to them the "one true church." The Jesuits and La Salle's Brothers of the Christian Schools were both very influential in the development of all Western education, not just Catholic education. They were extremely selective in their appointment of teachers and just as rigorous when it came to supervising them. The new interest in supervision, and the fact that it was carried out so carefully, went far to restore the image of the professional teacher. It also gave the teacher greater weight and authority in intellectual circles, even though the general population doubtlessly continued to believe that their children would learn more about the "right things" by staying home and working in the family business.

## Teachers in England

Eventually, the ideas put forth in the early years of the Reformation became united in many ways with those of humanism. The result was the emergence of a new image of education, schools, and teachers. The tremendous expansion and new respectability of the maturing occupation is well demonstrated by their manifestations in England and America. The earliest teachers of the English monastic schools had been so-called *secular clergy*. Although they were ordained priests, they worked wholly in worldly professions like teaching, rather than devoting themselves to a purely monastic life. Still, they were leading figures in the Catholic Church hierarchy. Some headmasters before the 14th century even had the authority to excommunicate. When Henry VIII broke relations with the Roman Catholic Church in the 16th century, many monastic schools disappeared. Henry set about the task of replacing them and finding new Anglican (Church of England) schoolmasters to operate them. It was a slow process, and for a while a few grammar schools had to carry on in place of the once-vast system of monastic schools.

The teaching profession in England had nearly disappeared by the end of the Reformation. Parents had taken over the duties of instructing their children in whatever they knew, usually business practices, social conventions, and religious obligations. Some parents continued to send their children to Anglican ministers, who taught a few students the rudiments of reading and religious doctrine, much as the chantry schoolmasters had once done. The wealthier children had private tutors, as before. Some housewives began to teach elementary school subjects to local pupils for a small fee. Teachers in these so-called *dame schools* were strictly private individuals who set themselves up to teach for a profit.

From the 15th century on, England's growing commercial class showed considerable interest in the education of its youngsters. Through its initiative secondary Latin grammar schools began to spring up everywhere. These were funded by joint endowments, often coming from what were known as *liveried companies*. It was upper-class merchants who gave impetus to the great *public schools* of England. These schools—Winchester, Eton, St. Paul's, Harrow, and others—were only "public" in the sense that the incomes derived from them became part of each school's treasury. Everyone was "free" to send their children to these institutions—but only if they paid the rather considerable tuition. The result, of course, was that only those of ample means became students at the public schools. Many poor children, especially those of superior intelligence, were granted scholarships in the spirit of Christian charity. But for the most part these schools were for children of the wealthy, who were preparing for high state and church positions.

The masters of these public schools were a rather powerful and sometimes petty lot who were determined (and employed) to carry forth the religious ideals of the Church of England, while at the same time fostering a familiarity with grammatical structures and literary classics, particularly in Latin. These masters were also hired to carry on the fine tradition of the school and its name, usually the name of the school's philanthropic founder, whether company or individual. Although this latter point may seem trivial, it was anything but that. Indeed, many public schools were endowed by wealthy persons who, in so doing, sought fame and perhaps immortality. The remembrance of their kind deeds was to be carried on in the school's name. Many of the original school charters specifically stated that available teaching positions should go to family members above all others.

The schoolmaster of the English public school was, in many ways, the model of the teaching professional in the 17th and 18th centuries throughout the Western world. He was almost always associated with entrenched religious interests, and was usually a minister himself. For many years, the most important function that he served—as with the chantry instructors—was the preparation of elaborate religious services to be sung in Latin on behalf of the school's founders and supporters. The master and

*Though often powerless, students sometimes revolted against tyrannical teachers, in fact as well as fiction. (Advertising woodcut for* School, *London and New York, 1869)*

his pupils engaged in long hours of choral training as a traditional way of honoring and expressing gratitude to—while indirectly contributing to the immortality of—the school's patron. A considerable portion of the teacher's time, then, was obsessed with the payment of a servile homage to a single individual. As patrons died or became less directly involved in the direction of the school and its operation, headmasters took over more of the administrative duties of the institution. In other situations, as when corporate groups of patrons offered company endowments, less attention was given to the praise and glory of one individual.

In any case, teachers eventually focused more on instruction in academic subjects and less on musical and religious ones. Where once a master was required to have a well-developed voice and to be able play a musical instrument, it eventually became more important that he be able to teach Latin grammar and literature, though with little emphasis on creative or intellectual aspects of the classics. The influence of humanism remained very strong in the Western world right up to the Industrial Age. The English schoolmasters taught mostly the Latin language. This occurred despite the fact that most of the students at these schools were from the wealthy families in business, whose sons were supposedly being educated for taking their part in the family enterprise.

A love of supervising and teaching children was one common thread throughout the development of the teaching profession—but zeal in punishment was another. The English schoolmaster was notorious for his love of punishing children. Nicholas Udall, a 16th century headmaster of Eton, was well known for his brutal techniques of reproach. Later schoolmasters there employed "holders down" while they administered the appropriate beatings. Instruments used became somewhat tamer in the 17th century, as witnessed by one comparatively humanistic recommendation that instructors use "a good sharp birchen rod and free from knots, for willow wands are insufferable." But at Charterhouse in the 18th century birch switches fastened

*In country or city, few teachers were noted for their tolerance. (From* Harper's New Monthly Magazine, *19th century)*

together for purposes of behavioral guidance were still "armed with buds as big as thorns, renewed after six strokes for fresh excoriation."

Punishment was to be meted out by alert instructors if they caught a student breaking house rules, such as closing his bedroom door (considered a sure sign of homosexual or self-erotic activity), going to the local ale house, or *not* smoking at defined intervals. Smoking was compulsory because it was thought to safeguard one against the plague.

Teachers were usually recruited from among graduates of the system itself, so that they were well versed from an early age in the workings and underlying philosophy of life and study at these boarding schools. That practice provided a sort of continuity of traditions and instructional curriculum and methods, but it also permitted a boring and self-defeating stagnation to set in. While pupils were drawn from the upper middle class for many years, the total emphasis on classical languages eventually turned these schools into private preserves for only the wealthiest of children. An increasing number of middle-class pupils began to turn toward the more practical studies that were available at the newer Puritan Dissenters' Academies. There they could learn mathematics, law, and other subjects related to business practice, as well as classical and even contemporary literature in the vernacular—in this case English.

## Colonial America

American schools were a sort of cross between the elite public schools and middle-class Dissenters' Academies. Many teachers were strictly bound to the traditional classical Latin instruction, especially at such outstanding establishments as the Boston Latin Grammar School, which opened in the 17th century. But there were other subjects to teach, especially in New England, where business and mercantile concerns were not only an economic concern but a religious one too. The Puritans who settled in New England were convinced that prosperity and hard work were sure signs of the grace of God. In the Southern colonies, settled more by gentlemen farmers than religious dissidents, teachers were more likely to follow the old English public school example of the sturdy, strict master who handed out all instruction in Latin.

The teaching profession in the New World was no more prestigious or prosperous than anywhere else at the time. Nonetheless, teachers were needed from the earliest of times. In 1642 the Massachusetts Bay Colony passed a law requiring that elementary instruction be made available to all children. Although parents could provide such instruction themselves or hire a tutor instead of sending their child to school, they had to be able to provide a certain minimum education. This included the reading of English, knowledge of civil laws, religious instruction, and apprenticeship in a trade. The need for trained teachers became increasingly evident, and in 1647 the Massachusetts legislature required each town of 50 families to provide an elementary school teacher, and each town of 100 families to establish also a Latin grammar school. Other colonies soon followed suit, and town elders and other municipal authorities were generally given the authority to hire and supervise teachers. For a time, towns shared teachers, who would journey from one to the other.

Teachers were responsible for seeing that all children became able to read and study the Bible. A familiarity with the Bible carried far more weight than any professional teaching credentials. Throughout the colonial period the American teacher was considered almost a missionary of the various Christian churches.

Few teachers considered their instructional work a full-time occupation, if only because it did not offer sufficient or regular income. Many teachers were not paid salaries at all but had to depend on gifts and tuitions, which were not always forthcoming. Often they were paid only with livestock or food; some were known to complain that they had so much of these goods that they would be better off operating a tavern than a school. Many teachers were ministers biding their time until they could be placed in a pastorate of their own, or lawyers waiting to obtain suitable employment in an established law firm. Others were employed on the side in just about every conceivable manner, most commonly ringing the town church bell and digging graves.

American teachers were licensed by civil authorities but were doggedly supervised by church selectmen. The most important qualification for teaching was religious orthodoxy, and the surest way to lose one's teaching job was to offer even slightly contrary views or subject matter. Children were sent to school to learn religion first and foremost, and reading, writing, and arithmetic only insofar as it pertained to the operation of the business or trade that they were likely to enter. Teachers, then, were expected to be of the highest moral character and to set the perfect example for the town children to follow. Like God and His ministers, they were to direct their flock with love and wisdom—but somehow relentless judgment and severity were more the Puritan norm. The Puritan town schools came to be called *public schools,* although they had almost nothing in common with the English public schools.

Some instructional employment was to be found in the American colonies at *private schools* and *academies.* Private schools were run by single headmasters who usually treated them as business enterprises as much as anything else. The most practical of educations was to be found in them, and teachers were recruited from the business world, as well as from the churches. Regardless of their own backgrounds, these teachers were hired to teach a purely secular curriculum to the middle-class students who filled these schools. The private school was eventually replaced by the corporate academy, run by a board of trustees like any other corporation. It was chartered by the state in which it operated but was free from the controls that were exercised over the town schools. Several outstanding academies had been established by the middle of the 18th century, among them the William Penn Charter School and Franklin's Academy in Pennsylvania, the Dummer Academy and Phillips Academy in Massachusetts, the Newark Academy in Delaware, the Washington Academy in New Jersey, and the Union School in Connecticut.

In the time of the Revolutionary War, teachers were still judged more for their religious orthodoxy and moral character than anything else—a practice roundly condemned by Benjamin Franklin. Their training was haphazard, often minimal, and certainly variable. Some barely knew how to read or write themselves, while others were distinguished speakers and skilled pedagogues, often educated in some of the finest colleges the New World had to offer. In general, teachers with the most education moved into the highest levels of the profession. A minimum amount of schooling would be required of an aspiring elementary school teacher, while the grammar school or secondary-level instructor would need to be well versed in the Latin as well as vernacular "classics." While many teachers were scolded for drunkenness and swearing, they were, as a group examples of proper conduct and virtuous behavior.

After the Revolution, districts achieved full legal autonomy over their own schools, first in New England and eventually throughout the new nation. These districts built their own schoolhouses, totally controlled the curriculum, and selected and appointed teachers to available positions. In the process, teaching finally passed out of the hands of the religious authorities, although the full impact of this change would not be realized until the 19th century.

A different pattern was being followed in the Catholic parts of the New World, in French Canada and in Central and South America. The first elementary school in the New World was actually founded in Mexico in 1525 by Catholic missionaries for Native American children. Throughout Latin America, missionaries pioneered in establishing schools. In large part their aim was to con-

*Country schoolmasters held school in rough quarters, often boarding with local families.* (*From* Harper's Monthly Magazine, *19th century*)

vert the Native Americans, but they also taught useful trades and skills. Secondary schools and universities were also established as time went on. Some of these were under lay control. But in colonial times the religious orders, especially the Dominicans and the Jesuits, played a dominant role in Latin American education. Education in South and Central America suffered grievously when these orders were expelled in the late 18th century.

In French Canada, education was at first less organized, given the small and dispersed population of the land. But there, too, the Catholic orders played an important role in establishing the first elementary and secondary schools and universities. Once the British took Canada, French support for these institutions dried up and education among the French population declined accordingly. Elsewhere in Canada, British-inspired patterns of education developed, much as they had in New England, but with wide provincial variations for a long time.

## A Time of Transition

In both Europe and America, and in both Protestant and Catholic countries, broad changes took place in the teaching profession between the time of the Reformation in the 16th century and the Industrial Revolution in the late 18th and 19th centuries. This transitional period bridges from the medieval notion of teaching as a purely sacred function (and hardly a sustaining profession at all) to the contemporary notion of teaching as a purely secular occupation. Basic changes in the perception of education and teaching were to have a profound effect on the modern developments within the profession and later—with the increasing influence of teachers—on the evolution of Western thought and even on the course of history itself.

The most significant change in this transitional period was the gradual shift in the control of education from the church to the state. Following the Reformation, the pathfinders of the new education sought financial aid and legal sanction from the state on the grounds that a people who had had intensive religious instruction would benefit all of society—and in secular as well as in sacred ways. While church authorities retained control over the early "public" forms of education, by the end of the 18th century many movements favored the total secularization of education. This cause was fueled largely by the increased emphasis on practical and vocational teaching that, in turn, had come about as a result of the Protestant work ethic. It had become something of a sacred act to do one's job as well as possible, and to prosper from it was a sure sign of the workings of Providence. Teachers, then, the argument went, ought to abandon their time-worn obsession with the classical literature and language of the Romans and attend to the commercial topics and vernacular "classics" instead.

But growth in the teaching profession was hindered by quarreling among factions within the Protestant movement. These were as damaging to the actual establishment of schools as was the more obvious struggle between Catholics and Protestants. As the great system of Catholic parish schools was largely destroyed—especially in Northern Europe—comparatively few schools arose to replace those abandoned. Universities preoccupied themselves with theological disputes in an age when scientific methodology and rationalism were making sweeping gains on medieval scholasticism. As a result, many scholars and students shunned these traditional bastions of higher learning to join scientifically based academies.

Teaching itself made little methodological progress during this period of transition. Professional training was scant, and most people who became teachers had never studied the art of teaching. In general, they followed the Christian dogma of the time, which emphasized that children were born sinful and that the good instructor (or parent or vocational master for that matter) should take pains to detect and drive away this evil. Physical punishment and mental discipline were the cornerstones of a teacher's instructional technique. Both punishment and discipline served to indoctrinate the pupil in the religious mores and customs of society. Punishment reminded a child of his inherent evil and his need to learn that which the schoolmaster proposed to instruct. It was not only good for the child's soul that he be whipped or knuckled on a fairly regular basis, but it was also good that he realize the underlying beneficence of such treatment. It was customary for a student to "thank" the master for the punishments he received. Verbal abuse and ridicule were also essential tools of the schoolmaster. It was during this era that the dunce's cap and dullard's stool came into vogue.

Discipline was the other primary instructional technique at the disposal of the typical teacher. This is seen not only in the curriculum development (or lack of it) during the period but also in the way in which information was to be digested by the pupil. Latin still formed the core of most secondary learning, although most elementary schools eventually introduced the vernacular instead, or sometimes in addition. The great fascination with Latin lay largely in the nature of the language. It was a difficult subject with elaborate declensions and grammatical structures that could be learned mainly through rote memorization, which demanded long hours of exacting study and practice. Teachers were happy to have a subject that could be so precisely monitored regarding levels of achievement and failure. Through Latin, they believed that they were training sharp minds; the idea was that students would one day be able to transfer this stringent mental discipline to other academic or occupational problems. Teachers became so obsessed with the significance of Latin for its own sake that there was little thought of education as a process of discovery, insight, and creativity. Francis Bacon, one of the new breed of rationalists and proponents of the scientific method, deplored the emphasis on "words, not matter" and urged in his *Advancement of Learning* that "other helps are required besides books."

While most teaching was dogmatic and stagnant, a great deal of dissension existed within the profession on the nature of teaching and the desirability of training. The Jesuits placed considerable emphasis on what we might now call behavioral or child psychology. They were quite concerned that the teachers they trained be able to encourage and stimulate children to learn, although they, too, believed that punishment and discipline were a necessary part of the occupation.

The Jesuits were foremost among the operators of what might be called teacher-training institutes. They demanded that their instructors be of high quality and keenly aware of different teaching strategies and techniques that were available. Moreover, they stressed learning as a creative and reasoning process, not only one of memorization, recall, and recitation.

Johann Pestalozzi operated several schools in Switzerland that were based on his intent to "psychologize education." He stressed the merits of physical education in conjunction with experiential and observational learning. He trained teachers in his schools to take care that their students might understand what they read and heard, rather than simply recall it word for word. John Sturm in Germany and the Moravian bishop Johann Comenius also shaped new ideas for the training of professional instructors.

Many of the new ideas regarding teacher training, curriculum, and methods were inspired by great writers of the 18th-century Enlightenment, such as Rousseau and Locke. They pointed the way to science and realism in education, based on the revolutionary notion that humans are good, rather than evil, by nature. These ideas were rarely put into practice and were not even necessarily well received in their day. But they laid the groundwork for the progressive movement that would alter the whole nature of the teaching profession in the 20th century.

Some advances based on these new ideas were made even in the 18th century, however. The Dissenters' Academies strongly opposed the classical and humanistic style of education. Greatly influenced by the work of Comenius, they offered courses in geography, history, and law, as well as high-level studies of vernacular literature and philosophy. Franklin's Academy in Philadelphia was in this mode.

Meanwhile, the German state of Prussia had risen to political prominence and promptly set about establishing one of the first truly national education systems. As early as 1713 laws were passed in Prussia requiring attendance of children at schools, which eventually came to be centrally organized and financed by the state. Not long after, part-time teaching was made illegal in order to develop a true professional class of instructors. A teacher-training institute was set up at Szczecin to standardize methods of instruction. By the end of the 18th century, all boys and girls between the ages of five and thirteen were compelled to attend school. Teachers had to be licensed by the state, a credential usually obtained after study and internships at one of the several teacher-training centers established for the purpose. Pestalozzian methods were widely adopted by the Prussian educational system, making it one of the best and most innovative in the world.

But these movements toward a stronger independent teaching profession were exceptions to the rule. Even by the end of the 18th century most teachers in the West were "trained" only by virtue of their familiarity with particular subject matter. They had no special learning in teaching methods or behavioral psychology.

Alongside general educators, there also existed *courtiers*. These were essentially private tutors to the aristocratic families within court society. The courtier was particularly important in the 16th century, when Castiglione's *The Courtier* and Elyot's *The Boke Named the Governor* were both presented as teacher's manuals of sorts for these distinctive tutors. Although relatively few in number, courtiers remained significant throughout

In addition to regular schooling, many students attended Sunday schools, often taught by volunteer religious teachers. (From Punch, or the London Charivari, 19th century)

the 16th, 17th, and 18th centuries because of the important and influential people they prepared for public life. Much of the instruction at this level was social, highlighting manners and customs of noble life, much as the knightly schools had done during the later Middle Ages. As dueling gained great popularity and respect in European court society, the courtier was obliged to teach this "subject" above all others. We might think this a rather shallow form of education, but the pupil's very life might well have depended on the skills obtained through such instruction. It was, even into the 19th century, a true "life skills" program.

In addition, many families outside court life, especially affluent families who lived on country estates, employed private tutors. These tutors were often young men whose funds or contacts were insufficient to take them into public or professional careers. But many were young women, themselves often home-educated, who were forced by circumstances to earn their living as *governesses*. Many a romantic novel has as its heroine a poor governess sent to teach children at an isolated manor house. Such novels often bring out the ambiguous position of private tutors—their breeding and education often obtained them a place at the family table or social affairs, but their status was considerably lowered by their being "hired help." This would be true even into the 20th century. No less a personage than Marie Sklodowska, later to become famous as the Nobel-prize-winning Marie Curie, spent some years of her youth as a governess—and was not allowed to marry the young man of the family for which she worked.

Perhaps the most significant factors in secularizing and popularizing education, while standardizing the preparation of teachers, were nationalism and democracy. Nationalism had led to the idea of national compulsory education in Prussia in the 18th century; most Western states did not develop similar systems until the 19th century. As for democracy, the idea that all people, regardless of birthright, could aspire to any earthly goal, was a great stimulant to universal and national education systems. Public education became a political necessity in England and especially in America, where—gradually and only with great struggle—all citizens came to have the right to vote. As Thomas Jefferson and other leaders in this movement were quick to point out—and as the early Greeks had been well aware—democracies could only be as good as the quality and availability of universal educational systems through which citizens could learn to be active participants in governing the state.

## After the Industrial Revolution

As the 19th century progressed, the Industrial Revolution had made even greater demands for the democratization of education. As urban manufacturing centers sprang up all over the Western world, there was a demand for a more sophisticated labor force. And as more people found jobs in the cities, the general standard of living began to rise, creating a much larger middle class. The result was a significantly increased interest in education.

The call for new schools and more teachers did not come—as it traditionally had—from the churches nor from the aristocrats, who had a vested interest in diverting social progress and political change. The call came from upper middle-class working people, who wanted their children to learn the current system of cultural values, to be sure, but also practical skills that would be useful to them in their future lives, especially in their occupations.

Scientific thought, the offspring of the Age of Reason and the Enlightenment, further changed the focus of education during the Industrial Revolution and the Age of Invention. Together with the new mood of nationalism, it brought about more and more secular control over education. The Prussians led the way here, too. In 1808 a Department of Public Instruction was formed. Eventually, the *Realschule* (Realist School), with its more scientific-oriented curriculum, replaced the classical *Gymnasium* as the chief type of secondary school. In France, by 1833, local communities were charged with maintaining their own elementary schools. Although these schools were still primarily church-related for a while, they eventually adopted more practical and scientific curricula as they passed into the hands of municipal and local authorities.

Schools in the United States were the least sectarian by the middle of the 19th century. Local "common" schools had become widely accepted, and private schools—most of which had church ties—had largely declined. Education in America had become more purely public and free from religious or aristocratic control than anywhere else in the world. There were public high schools (secondary schools) as early as 1821 and the first state board of education was instituted in Massachusetts in 1837. Public secondary schools were not common in Europe before the 20th century. They are still poorly developed in England, where the elitist "public" (what Americans would call private) schools were the chief means of postelementary education right up into recent decades.

Beyond contributing to the secularization of education, scientific thought also changed the schools themselves. The curriculum became more down to earth, including courses in geography, mathematics, biology, and even some vocational studies, like woodworking and printing. For the most part, though, curricular developments tended to retain the pure sciences, while the vocational crafts were relegated to separate, generally private "vocational" schools.

The trends in scientific thought also led to new ideas about children and their place in society, about teaching as an attainable art based on methodological studies and innovations, and about learning as a psychological and even sociological process, which can be assisted or hindered by various instructional approaches. One of the most profound effects of the Industrial Revolution was that people demanded that education produce a technologically and commercially sophisticated work force. Schools were pressed to put aside religious studies in favor of practical ones. Early in the 19th century American elementary schools even began to forbid religious teaching in the classroom, although such restrictions had only token adherence for many years to come. With the sanction of the state, secular education was rapidly becoming a more solidifying and potent force in Western society than the churches.

As new states began to rise in Europe, they used education as the basis for teaching their people various ideologies and patriotic obligations. Teachers were a tool in this mission and in the long-term goal of achieving national supremacy. The Prussian state was again the model of this new statehood married to education. Its schoolmasters had been trained in teacher's seminaries (making even neater the parallel between teachers in state schools and the clergy within the churches) as early as the 18th century. Frederick the Great later made this training a prerequisite of professional teaching, except for retired soldiers who were considered the most perfect sort to hold such positions. Teachers were taught to train armies of citizens who would make Prussia the leading state of Europe through any means available. The system was a model of the education-in-service-of-the-state idea that was soon to dominate the Western World.

## The Non-Western World

In the East, education had long been viewed in terms of state service. From ancient times Chinese schools had been used to train aspiring government officials, and Japanese schools developed in the same manner. Indian education had always been dominated more by religious authorities than by the concerns of the state. But in none of these systems was there a notion of mass education. Schooling was strictly for the aristocratic classes of society, who used it for attaining church or state positions, so maintaining the social and political status quo.

By the 19th century these static and elitist educational systems of the Eastern countries had generally fallen into decline. At the same time they were being influenced by Western ideas and examples. India was an integral part of the British Empire at this time, and so its system was actually remodeled along Western lines.

Although Westernization often meant modernization and the introduction of the sciences, it also often assumed the superiority of Western culture over Eastern. The British "modernization" of the Indian educational system meant institutionalization of intensive training for a handful of Indians so that they could work within the British-Indian bureaucracy. The aim was to defuse nationalism, by showing that opportunities did, in fact, exist for Indians willing to work within the structure of the empire, rather than struggling to dissolve it. Ironically, some of the few Indian intellectuals so educated later became leaders of the independence movement that finally ousted the British from India in the 20th century.

The same pattern emerged elsewhere in the East and in Africa as well. Much as their earlier Catholic

*At many times and places, elementary school students have been regarded as the special province of women teachers. (From Harper's Monthly Magazine, 19th century)*

counterparts had done, Protestant missionaries founded schools wherever they took their ministries. Clearly education was the readiest way to bring new ideas—both religious and secular—to non-Christian peoples. Those who received Western-style educations, at elementary and secondary mission schools and sometimes in European or American universities, often later led the fight for independence in their homelands. Chou En-lai, a major figure in the Chinese Communist revolution, for example, studied in a mission school in China and furthered his education in France, England, and Germany before returning to political action in China.

Throughout the East in the 19th century, only a handful of privileged youths received any education. The masses of people were not only unschooled but completely illiterate. By the beginning of World War I only an estimated 10 percent of all Indians could read or write. The situation was little better in China, Japan, or elsewhere in the East. The teaching profession in this part of the world, then, was understandably under-developed, crude, and barely influential at all. There were private tutors, but they worked essentially as individuals rather than as members of a cohesive professional class. There were also officially appointed instructors, whose main job was to teach students bare facts. This was particularly the case in China, where the centuries-old merit system, based on civil service examination, was still in use. Teachers were little more than monitors in such a context, helping pupils to prepare for specific exams.

## Professionalism

It was in the Western world that the effects of the 19th century's scientific and industrial changes were most profound. With sharply increasing student enrollments at state and local schools, there was a call for better trained and more purposefully prepared schoolmasters. Changing living conditions—urbanization, factory life, rapid transportation, and the like—all affected the content of instruction, bringing about transformation of curricula. New social sciences, notably psychology, gave fresh insight into child behavior and appropriate teaching techniques. There was a new interest in elementary, and even infant, education. Long considered a crude necessity in taming the unruly spirits of young people, elementary teaching began to be considered a meaningful stepping stone to higher forms of learning. For the first time, it became common to actually prepare elementary schoolmasters for their jobs—not only in subject matter, but in instructional methods as well. With the increased demand for professionally trained teachers, salaries, standards of living, and social status within the occupation were bound to improve. By the end of the 19th century there were clear improvements on these grounds. But because teachers had to go through more extensive (and expensive) training and career preparation, they were beginning to complain more loudly than ever about underpayment, long hours, and lack of respect.

The Prussians had been the first to train teachers in any organized and systematic manner. In their militaristic teaching seminaries, they developed a scheme for measuring the success of trainees, introducing a special qualifying exam, which a person had to pass in order to be a licensed teacher. One major change in the movement to train teachers in Prussia was the rapid development in scope and significance of the elementary school in the 19th century. Seeing schooling as important to their youth, the Prussians carefully inspected and upgraded this long neglected level of learning. Since education was an arm of the state, these teachers—traditionally ill-prepared and barely literate themselves—became the focus of sweeping reform. This reform began with intensive training to insure that teachers would instill nationalistic zeal and patriotism in the state's upcoming generations. Considering Prussia's startling ascendancy to world power, its stunning victory in the Franco-Prussian War, and its subsequent creation of an impressive empire, it is not surprising that teacher training soon became important elsewhere. After all, the Prussians themselves largely credited their educational system for their achievements.

Teacher training first began in France under Napoleon in 1810. He established the Superior Normal School to prepare secondary-level teachers for the *lycée* and *college*. The training of elementary teachers soon gained attention, too, and in 1833 legislation was passed providing each French department with primary normal (teacher education) schools. Graduation from a primary school was the only requirement for entrance into one of the "normals," since it was properly asssumed that anyone who had an education beyond that would have little interest in a teaching career, especially at the primary level.

At first the training courses in the normal schools stressed innovative teaching methods, like those of Pestalozzi, but conservative and reactionary political forces quickly condemned such practices as dangerous to the stability of the Republic. The countless revolutions and general unrest that stalked all of Europe, and particularly France, in the middle of the 19th century was thought by conservative factions to be rooted in new philosophies and democratic ideals of education. Teachers were immediately suspect, and their training was stripped of all creativity. They were to be schooled only in subject matter and were to teach only concrete information and operations. The most important curriculum at hand, the conservatives believed, was that founded on the preservation of the existing government. Teachers were to be prepared strictly in conformity with the ideals of patriotism as set forth and closely supervised by the Ministry of Public Instruction.

This would last into the 20th century. In 1941 the French primary normal schools were abolished by the Vichy government, puppet of the German Nazi occupiers. These schools were not reinstated until after the war under the Fourth Republic. During this period, philosophy instructors had their tenures terminated, Jewish teachers were largely barred from obtaining professional certification, and teaching was viewed as a potentially traitorous occupation, strictly subject to government review. Not surprisingly, a number of teachers' organizations eventually joined underground resistance movements that helped overthrow the Vichy.

The normal school movement in America had similar limitations, but at least it marked a considerable improvement over the private academies that had previously undertaken the major share of the teacher-training task. The academies had stressed theological beliefs and specific subject preparation almost exclusively. They were also far too expensive for students preparing for a low-paying job like teaching. The normal schools, by contrast, were publicly supported (and therefore more affordable) institutions created to train secular teachers for the most rapidly expanding publicly supported educational system in the world.

The first public normal school was established in Lexington, Massachusetts, in 1839, but it was—like the whole normal school movement in America—looked upon with considerable disfavor in the beginning. Many people were opposed to the notion that a democratic nation had to submit—as had the autocratic nations of Prussia and France—to state control of teacher training. Was the United States training an army of educated puppets who would blind their students to all except whatever was sanctioned by the state? Not so, said Charles Brooks, who popularized the pro-normal slogan "As is the teacher so is the school" in his ardent appeals on behalf of better-quality teacher preparation.

Indeed, the American normal schools were not as politically controlled as those of Europe. They were more open to the new social sciences and the information they brought to bear on the educational process. By the end of the 19th century they had undergone profound changes in focus due to various movements. The "Oswego movement" of the 1860's, based in the state normal school at Oswego, New York, stressed Pestalozzianism. The later Herbartian movement was centered in the state normal school at Normal, Illinois. The latter was based on the ideas of the early 19th-century German educator, Johann Friedrich Herbart. He emphasized the roles of motivation and interest in the learning process, rather than the boring and repetitive drilling technique that was still common.

The new ideas and methods taught at the normal school, superficial and narrow as they may seem by contemporary standards, represented a marked improvement in teaching strategies. Only a short time before this, the monitorial method taught by Joseph Lancaster at a Philadelphia teacher training school had dominated the scene of methodological innovation. The monitorial system provided that the teacher instruct *monitors*—chosen pupils; they would, in turn, act as teachers to other students in the class. The method was at first hailed as a great practical device. Hundreds of students could crowd a public hall and be taught in rows, at the heads of which there was an appointed monitor. This mass-production education was quickly derailed by more sensitive educators. But it did illustrate the need for new group teaching methods to replace the older hearing-recitation method, whereby the teacher of the one-room schoolhouse had to individually instruct and test each student. Of course, group instruction was impossible in such a situation, because there were no classes or grade levels by which groups could be known to have a fairly similar frame of reference and history of preparation.

Schools were growing fastest in America, because of the democratic commitment to mass education. As a result, the training of teachers eventually became the leading concern in the profession. As early as 1839 Professor Andrew J. Yates had insisted that teachers should have a more liberal education than the provincial training afforded by professional schools. He thought no one should be allowed to teach unless he was a graduate from an academy in which pedagogy was properly taught by a university graduate. He envisioned departments of "public instruction" in the universities themselves. Teachers had traditionally not been required to have a very broad or extensive education, but Yates'

*After the American Civil War, many New England "school-marms" went south to open schools for newly freed black students. (Library of Congress)*

views were to be realized before the end of the century. Horace Mann taught a course at Antioch College of Ohio in 1852 entitled "Didactics of Theory and Art of Teaching." Between 1856 and 1873, the University of Iowa conducted a Normal Department, and Illinois Normal University was established in 1857. In 1888, the New York College of Teachers (later renamed Teachers' College, Columbia University) was established. Seven years later John Dewey began his enormously influential educational instruction at the University of Chicago. State teachers' colleges were established and eventually teachers would be trained exclusively at the universities and colleges. But this final development did not really flower until the 20th century.

Besides the rise of elementary education, perhaps the most significant occurrence in the profession during the 19th century was the increase of women teachers, partly because of the new importance placed on primary schools. As early as the 17th and 18th centuries there had been so-called *dame schools*, in which ladies would take care of a group of children in their homes for a stated fee. These "schools" were essentially caretaker affairs, and the teachers themselves were little qualified for any instruction beyond simple grammar. By the early 19th century the *infant school* became popular, and women usually undertook their private organization and operation.

Men had never been much interested in elementary education, partly because it was so closely associated with the concept of motherhood and partly because it paid so poorly. Many educators felt that teaching at primary levels was best handled by women, since so much patience and "mothering" were required. Women were generally given credit for little intellectual capacity and were regarded as well suited to teaching the boring, unchallenging primary curriculum. In a formal sense, this was even somewhat true, since women rarely had an education that extended beyond elementary school. In addition, women were paid lower salaries than men. That was another reason why they were the preferred employees at the primary levels. By the end of the century, the status of the woman instructor in the United States at least had so improved that the difference in salaries between men and women largely disappeared.

The feminization of teaching was easily the greatest in North America—both the United States and Canada—where public schools overflowed with enrollees. With the early 1800's migrations into the Western frontier, women were used—as they long had been—increasingly to teach summer school sessions, while their male counterparts were busy working the fields. Eventually women began to teach winter school sessions, too. By the middle of the century several leading educators—notably Horace Mann and Henry Barnard—depended on women to staff their winter schools. Barnard felt that women were superior teachers, partly because, he believed, they were of a more predictable (and inevitably higher) moral character than men with similar educational preparation.

As scores of men marched off to battle during the Civil War (from which many failed to return), there were more teaching vacancies than ever. Women filled them eager-

*Buildings like this church were sometimes pressed into service as schools. (Maryland, 1938) (By Arthur Rothstein, from* The Depression Years, *Dover, 1978)*

ly. Up to that time, they were allowed to work in only a few occupations, teaching being one of the foremost. By the end of 1880, they made up 57 percent of the professional ranks. This figure grew to 70 percent by the end of the century and 85 percent just after World War I. This change has not been repeated elsewhere in the Western world to this day, where male teachers generally continue to dominate.

The 19th century had seen the beginning of changes in the teaching profession. But most innovations were confined to strictly limited or experimental circumstances and did not apply generally. At the turn of the 20th century, teachers were better paid, in relation to other occupations, than they had been 100 years earlier. However, they also had to be much better prepared and schooled. That meant higher career investments in terms of both time and money. Teachers in urban areas were much better paid than those in rural areas, where education often had progressed little. Although new pedagogical techniques and psychologies of the child were developing, schoolmasters were still typically harsh with their punishments and medieval in their methods. Children were still severely beaten in most schools, including those in England, France, and America. Instruction was delivered primarily on an individual basis in one-room schoolhouses, where students were not separated into grades. Only some of the larger urban areas, such as New York, Chicago, and London, had opened schools where instructors could teach in grade levels, thereby permitting them to instruct a whole group at one time.

Rote memorization of texts remained the chief means of learning, and hearing recitations was still the primary means by which students were evaluated. Although the physical and social sciences, physical education, and even the fine arts were gradually being introduced into curricula, studies of the classics and religious instruction were not only retained but endured as the basic selections on the educational menu. Even in America, where religion had supposedly been separated from the public schools by law, it remained the basis of most learning. Reputable moral and religious standing was still the chief qualifying factor for the successful teacher.

Although teacher training had been formalized and improved to a laudable extent, most professional teachers remained poorly prepared. Many women who taught elementary school in America had been trained only in "academies" that were nothing more than upper levels of instruction attached to typical primary schools. Many others learned the art only through short apprenticeship periods. Although teachers' salaries had improved, they generally were still far below those of other professional workers. This was due in part to the influx of women into the profession, but even more to the continuing low status of teachers.

## Modern Teachers

The 19th century had seen the evolution of teaching as a full-time occupation for both men and women. The movements that had begun to improve the quality of the profession were continued into the 20th century, giving rise to an entirely new image and status of the teacher after World War I. Some underlying social changes permitted the breakthrough in the occupation's maturity.

Advances in the social sciences, notably psychology, have had a profound impact on the current views of childhood and the educational task. Children have become more respected as individuals and as learners. Researchers and practitioners in the field of clinical psychology have shown the importance of childhood to the eventual shaping of the adult. Sigmund Freud, one of the earliest of these researchers, pointed out the significance of sexual identification and aggression in the developmental stages of early childhood. Such pioneer work made available new explanations for human behavior that were not tied to religious perspectives.

Meanwhile, other experimenters and theorists were more accurately isolating and defining the learning experience itself. Such studies generally tended to support a model of learning as a genuine transaction between the teacher and student rather than—as had usually been presumed—a process whereby the teacher gave information and the student simply absorbed it, much as a sponge might absorb a puddle of water. It was found that the very behaviors of both student and teacher—learning and teaching—might be modified and restructured scientifically so as to maximize the benefits of the educational situation. Clearly, the 20th-century teacher would need to be better trained in the techniques of behavioral management than ever before, particularly as the student was increasingly accepted as an active, rather than passive, agent in the instructional process.

Education itself has been transformed by modern social views. Schools in the United States once were routinely segregated by race. But under social pressure, backed by the federal government, they are increasingly being integrated—both in students and faculty—even though housing patterns and prejudice continue to foster segregation. Minority groups also have been treated with somewhat more respect. In countries with large immigrant populations, the pattern once was to force all peoples to drop their old culture and language for that of their new land. But more recently, some schools in countries with large ethnic minority groups have turned more toward bilingual education, following the lead of Canada with its very large French population. The problem with that, however, is that the students are not then fully prepared to enter the social mainstream.

The industrialization and urbanization of modern society has resulted in a multiplication of occupations, suboccupations, and para-occupations, which have vastly increased the need for more specific and practical courses of instruction. More generally, the commercial expansion of the world has made education more responsive to the demand for technically competent and sophisticated citizens to fit the industrialized mode of society—to work in its factories, operate its machinery, and finance its propulsion to ever greater heights. As the material and commercial wealth of the world has grown rapidly, so has the preference for scientific and materialistic philosophies and doctrines. One result of this has been the widespread abandonment of both church and home as the primary educational institutions. Their replacement has become the public, nonsectarian—in fact, nonreligious—school systems that characterize most education in modern nations.

Many states and nations still see public schools as a means of promoting national unity, patriotism, and the overall supremacy of the state. This was clearly recognized in Nazi Germany in the 1930's, when Hitler made the educational system a handmaiden to his political plots and racist prejudices. Taking control of the schools, he approved the use of only a handful of textbooks that coincided with his views, and he selected those whom he wanted to hold teaching posts. Manipulative use of education and teachers is seen today in the Soviet Union, the People's Republic of China, and many other totalitarian and authoritarian countries. Teachers in these countries are carefully prepared and chosen, and only those deemed representative of the aims and philosophies of the state may hope for fruitful careers.

Even in the democratic nations of the world, education is regarded—although perhaps to a smaller and less visible degree—as a tool of the state. After the Soviet Union's successful launch of its space satellite Sputnik I in 1957, some people began saying that American teachers had become too humanitarian and concerned for the welfare of the child. They blamed teachers for "losing the edge" in the education race. There were immediate calls for improved instruction in science and technology in the United States, as a reaction against schooling that had "gone soft." The back-to-basics program that stressed science and mathematics, aimed at reestablishing America as the leading world power, was summarized by the popular 1960's slogan "the pursuit of excellence." During the Vietnam War, conservative interests decried the failure of teachers—especially those in higher education—to instill patriotic fervor for American troops fighting in Southeast Asia.

The communistic and democratic forms of education differ somewhat in the evaluation of a student's achievements. In democratic systems, achieved academic status is generally based on the intellectual development of each individual student. In the communist nations achieved status is more often based on nationalistic goals and standards, which sometimes eclipse regard for scholarship or objective research. But in general, achieved status based on educational accomplishment has, in the 20th century, largely replaced the ascribed status of earlier times, which was based solely on birthright. This may be partly attributed to the contemporary emphasis on scientific and rational thought, which has become commonplace in the educational arena.

For many centuries teaching was the tool of religion, and in some ways and in some countries it still is. But since modern times the profession has come to be viewed more as the servant of the state—and most recently sometimes as the implement of science. Science now forms the basis of teacher training, instruction, and evaluation. The 20th century has seen remarkable changes in the profession. The typical educational curriculum is now rooted in practical problem solving, rather than memorization and mental discipline.

As early as the late 19th century, John Dewey was questioning the assumption that teaching through discipline was "good for the mind." He thought of the teacher as more of a director of student activities and discoveries, which remained above all the student's *own* activities and discoveries. This new role model for the classroom instructor was popularized after World War I by William Kirkpatrick, who trained schoolteachers at Columbia University's Teachers' College in New York. This new view of the classroom as an experience in democracy, involving the student's exploration of his or her individuality, became the groundwork of the *progressive movement*. This has revolutionized the role of the teacher, even though the progressive ideal of teaching has come under fire during times of extreme nationalism. At such times teaching has occasionally been regarded as highly suspect or even subversive to the extent that it undermines patriotism and national unity in the name of humanitarianism and individualism.

Teaching has become a polished profession. Sophisticated training has become commonplace, as even elementary school teachers are now generally required to hold university or college degrees. Whole university departments and colleges have been developed exclusively toward achieving the goal of excellence in teaching, developing technological aids and innovative methods, such as team teaching and in-service workshops. In the great age of specialization, teaching as a profession has become more particularly defined than ever before. Instructors are trained not only on various grade levels but also in particular subjects and methods of teaching. Auxiliary personnel have also been trained to aid in the teaching process—*librarians, reading* and

*This grade-school teacher has yet to capture the attention of the young student in the front row. (Maryland, 1938) (By Arthur Rothstein, from* The Depression Years, *Dover, 1978)*

*speech specialists, psychologists*, and the like. These jobs are held by people who are not only professionals in their own right but are specialized in performing their duties in school settings.

More recently, teachers have organized into a powerful labor force. Even in the late 19th century, there was a popular trend toward establishing teacher "associations," to bring the professionals together to discuss their common practices, directions, and goals.

In the 20th century *teachers' unions* were formed, despite the popular notion that teachers should avoid contractual and labor disputes because they were employed partly as role models for children. In the 1960's these unions reached unprecedented levels of militancy, as a wave of *teacher strikes* temporarily closed schools in many parts of the Western world. Today, these unions are among the most powerful and influential labor organizations. Teachers now enjoy improved salary and benefit contracts, for only partial work years. Lower levels of teaching still have less repute than the higher ones. The sharpest distinction on these grounds lies between the school teachers (elementary and secondary grades) and the higher education (college and university) professors, who in some respects are more properly regarded in another category altogether, that of *scholar*.

Besides having better salaries, teachers today have better benefit plans and raises scheduled according to accumulated experience and additional training. Elementary and secondary school teachers are often now paid on the same salary scale. Women still dominate the elementary school teaching profession in North America, though slightly less so than in the past. But elsewhere in the world men are the dominant professional force at all levels of education. Generally speaking, the higher the level of teaching, the greater the degree of subject specialization and the smaller the amount of teacher training. At the highest levels of instruction there is virtually no training in behavioral psychology or teaching methods. The idea behind this situation is apparently this: the elementary teacher is obliged to instill in the pupil the desire to learn, while the secondary teacher (and later, the university professor) need only present information relevant to a particular subject. The students are presumed by that time to be able to learn on their own without further instructional aid other than is available in the textbooks. The highest levels of teaching, then, are most inclined toward a subject-centered approach, while the lowest levels have a more student-centered approach. The pendulum tends to swing somewhat. Some in education are reassessing the heavy emphasis on teacher training and are seeking to attract those teachers who are best trained in their particular subjects. This is especially true in private schools, as opposed to public schools, in America.

Teacher shortages were a real problem in the early 1960's in the United States. More recently, even though teaching is the largest of the professions, there is a considerable surplus of teachers, except in some highly technical fields. Shortages loom again in the future, however. Teachers are protected after a few years of service by *tenure*, under which it becomes virtually impossible to fire or replace them except for the most flagrant abuses. The teaching profession as a whole—as is usually the case with vested interest groups—tends to be conservative about itself and adverse to change. This assures a certain continuity within education but prevents consideration of more innovative and experimental forms of teaching. Many teachers, unable or unwilling to learn better methods of teaching or evaluation, prefer to employ elaborate testing and evaluation procedures designed to constantly categorize students and quantify their progress, avoiding the real task of instruction and the development of learning experiences. In all fairness, however, this obsession with evaluation is often welcomed and even insisted on by school boards and administrations.

In America creative forms of teaching are more commonly encouraged at private schools. For this reason, many high-quality teachers prefer to seek employment at these institutions, where they are unfettered by the bureaucratic, administrative, and political demands placed on the public-school teacher. Although private-school teachers are usually paid less and enjoy fewer benefits and far less security, they are also often able to be less inhibited, more creative, and less subject to a newly recognized professional hazard—teacher burnout.

In addition to teachers of the standard modern curriculum, many helpers and specialists aid in the educational enterprise, usually as part of the staff at schools. They include *teaching assistants, guidance counselors, psychologists, reading specialists, physical education instructors, vocational instructors, art teachers, music teachers, special education teachers, speech therapists*, and teachers of the gifted. Most of these specialties are very new to the educational scene, but some have their roots deep in history.

Perhaps the oldest of them is the *music teacher*, who has been important since early Greek times. In medieval Christian schools, music was a major part of the curriculum. Under the guidance of their music teacher, students often sang hymns during the Sunday mass. Musical instruction was an important subject in church-related schools, especially in the chantry schools, which were founded for the express purpose of training students to sing masses for their benefactors.

*Physical education* also has roots in ancient Greece. *Art education* became significant during the Renaissance, when the ideal of the well-rounded individual preoccupied the humanistic educators. After the Reformation both of these specialties lost a great amount of their appeal, especially in Calvinist schools, where music, dance, and even many forms of art were thought to be evil manifestations. The Protestant schools did contribute to the rising importance of *vocational instruction*, though, particularly with the onset of the Commercial and Industrial Revolutions of modern times. If medieval or Renaissance schools included music, dance, art, physical education or vocational instruction in their curricula, these subjects were invariably taught by the same instructor who handled courses in English, Latin, and mathematics.

*Guidance* and *vocational counseling* have their roots in the Greek system of appointing a *pedagogue* for each school boy. The pedagogue followed the student to and from school, made sure he was doing his work and getting his assignments, and supervised his moral and social development. In more modern times, *tutors* were commonly hired to assist and guide pupils at the English "public" schools. Each of these tutors worked with a particular boy, whose parents made the arrangements and paid the fee.

The first formal system of professional guidance in an educational capacity came in America. In 1882 President Daniel Coit Gilman of Johns Hopkins University appointed a board of advisers to insure that every student "may have a friend to consult in the perplexities which arise." With the increasing complexity of the industrial world and the expanding multitude of occupational categories available to students, the Boston School Committee in 1909 began a program of vocational guidance within the city's public schools. In the following year Harvard University began offering some professional training in the field, and by 1913 the National Vocational Guidance Association was organized.

Guidance counselors today are specifically prepared and must often be licensed members of guidance associations and hold university degrees in counseling within educational settings. The trend has spread to both public and private school systems throughout the world. In many countries the state appoints counselors to be sure that national quotas in specific occupational slots are being properly maintained according to predetermined guidelines.

Teachers today, owing largely to their historical roots in ministries of various sorts, are still employed with the understanding that they be of high moral character and proper role models. For this reason, there is frequently

*Male teachers are still some-thing of a rarity in elementary schools. (American Federation of Teachers, AFL-CIO)*

bitter controversy over the appointment of an open homosexual or atheist. As the family unit in the Western world has deteriorated, and as the churches' authority over the secular lives of people has diminished, teachers are increasingly called upon to mold high moral character and good citizenship. This is a particularly important role in areas where both parents are often working and thus rely increasingly on the school system to bring up their child. When problems like delinquency or underachievement develop in some children, teachers are often blamed for their failure to produce suitable children, students, and citizens. The teacher today is often called upon to be instructor, parent, and priest all at once.

For related occupations in this volume, *Scholars and Priests*, see the following:
Librarians
Monks and Nuns
Priests
Scholars
School Administrators

For related occupations in other volumes of the series, see the following:
in *Artists and Artisans*:
    Calligraphers
in *Communicators*:
    Authors
    Publishers and Booksellers
    Scribes
in *Healers* (forthcoming):
    Physicians and Surgeons
    Psychologists and Psychiatrists
in *Leaders and Lawyers*:
    Lawyers
    Judges
in *Performers and Players*:
    Athletes
    Dancers
    Musicians
in *Scientists and Technologists*:
    Biologists
    Chemists
    Geographers
    Geologists
    Mathematicians
    Physicists
in *Warriors and Adventurers*:
    Soldiers

# Suggestions for Further Reading

For further information about the occupations in this family, you may wish to consult the books below.

## Curators

Burns, William A. *Your Future in Museums*. New York: Richards Rosen Press, Inc., 1967. An interesting, straightforward account of the present-day staffing of museums.

Katz, Herbert, and Marjorie Katz. *Museums, U.S.A.* Garden City, New York: Doubleday, 1965. A good survey of contemporary American museums and related occupations, including an introductory chapter on the historical development of museums in the U.S. and a helpful bibliography of both primary and secondary sources.

Thomson, Peggy. *Museum People: Collectors and Keepers at the Smithsonian*. Englewood Cliffs, New Jersey: Prentice-Hall, 1977. First-hand interviews with a wide assortment of employees of the Smithsonian Institution in Washington, D.C.

## Librarians

Hessel, Alfred. *A History of Libraries*. Translated by Reuben Peiss. New Brunswick, New Jersey: Scarecrow Press, 1955. A very thorough tracing of the historical development of libraries, with some interesting notes on the growth of librarianship.

Johnson, Elmer D. *A History of Libraries in the Western World*. New York: Scarecrow Press, 1965. An extremely interesting and exhaustive treatment of the history of libraries, including many references to the profession of librarian and excellent bibliographical notes.

## Priests, Monks, and Nuns

Eastwood, Charles Cyril. *Life and Thought in the Ancient World*. Philadelphia: Westminster Press, 1964. A classic look at the ancient foundations of religions.

Gard, Richard A., ed. *Buddhism*. New York: George Braziller, 1962. A good, basic study of Buddhism and its professional leadership through the ages.

Heimert, Alan. *Religion and the American Mind: From the Great Awakening to the Revolution*. Cambridge,

Massachusetts: Harvard University Press, 1966. A scholarly study that offers some perspective on the role of the religious professions in Colonial America.

James, Janet Wilson, ed. *Women in American Religion.* Philadelphia: University of Pennsylvania Press, 1980. Scholarly readings on the role of women in religion throughout American history; contains especially good sections on missionaries, sisterhoods, and women in the ministry.

Leuba, James H. *The Reformation of the Churches.* Boston: Beacon Press, 1950. Considers changes in the church during the Reformation; Chapter 6, "Tradition in the Churches," is especially on target, taking up the issue of how clergy are and ought to be trained.

Lucas, Lawrence. *Black Priest/White Church: Catholics and Racism.* New York: Random House, 1970. Illustrates the issue of racism in the contemporary Catholic priesthood.

Morris, Hames. *The Preachers.* New York: St. Martin's, 1973. A look at some of the fiery mass media preachers in contemporary America.

Renou, Louis, ed. *Hinduism.* New York: George Braziller, 1962. A good, basic study of Hinduism and its professional leadership through the ages.

Sinclair, Upton. *The Profits of Religion.* New York: Vanguard, 1918. A classic, irreverent view of the religious professions, considered as somewhat insincere, corrupt, and money-hungry.

Walker, Williston. *A History of the Christian Church.* New York: Scribner's, 1959. A good general background history of the church and its vocations.

Wise, Carroll A. *Pastoral Counseling: Its Theory and Practice*. New York: Harper, 1951. A look at the rising 20th-century importance of counseling in the ministerial professions.

## Teachers and Scholars

Brubacher, John S. *A History of the Problems of Education*, 2nd ed. New York: McGraw-Hill, 1966. A broad variety of topical issues are confronted vividly in this well-documented and thought-provoking volume.

Butts, Freeman R. *A Cultural History of Western Education: Its Social and Intellectual Foundations*, 2nd ed. New York: McGraw-Hill, 1955. An extensive account of the history of education and the professions that have developed along with it.

Eby, Frederick. *The Development of Modern Education*, 2nd ed. Englewood Cliffs, New Jersey: Prentice-Hall, 1952. A lively, colorful view of the development of education and its related occupations since the Renaissance.

Gathorne-Hardy, Jonathan. *The Old School Tie: The Phenomenon of the English Public School*. New York: Viking Press, 1977. A bright anecdotal account of English public schools, including startling and enlightening insights into the roles played by the headmasters and the instructors.

Haskins, Charles Homer. *The Rise of Universities*. Ithaca and London: Cornell University Press, 1957; reprint of 1923. A brief but delightful portrait of medieval students and professors at university.

Rudolph, Frederick. *The American College and University*. New York: Vintage Books, 1962. An in-depth look at American higher education, with some fine sections on administrators and faculties.

Ryan, Patrick J. *Historical Foundations of Public Education*, 2nd ed. Dubuque, Iowa: William C. Brown, 1968. A nicely illustrated summary of public education from its inception, with frequent references to leaders and the rise of educational professions.

# Index

Abbasid caliphs, 9
*Address to the Nobility*
  (Luther), 146
*Advancement of Learning*
  (Bacon), 160
*Agape*, 62
Age of the Hundred
  Schools; 98, 117
Akhenaton, 43
Alexander the Great 95
Alexandria, Egypt, 1,
  7, 96
*Amarius*, 9
American Association of
  Museums, 5
Anglican Church, 149
Apostles, 62
Apostolic Age, 63
Apostolic succession
  doctrine, 65
Aquinas, St. Thomas, 23
Archbishop, 66
Aristophanes, 8
Aristotle, 95, 97
Art education, 183
Ascetics, 21, 52-53, 67-68
Ashmolean Museum,
  Oxford, 2
Astrologers, 35
Athens, 118-119
*Augures*, 47-48
Authority, issue of, 104
*Ayatollah*, 90

Babylonian Captivity, 58-59
Bacchus cult, 49
Bacon, Francis, 159-160
Baptism, 63

Barnard, Henry, 110, 174
Barnum, P.T., 4
Benedictine monks, 22
Benedictine Rule, 22, 25
Berlin, University of, 102
Bhakti cults, 67-68
Bible, 142, 154
Bilingual education, 177
Bishops, 64, 88
Bodley, Sir Thomas, 11-12
*Boke Named the
  Governor, The*
  (Elyot), 161
*Book of the Dead*, 38-39
Boston Athenaeum, 13
Boston Latin Grammar
  School, 153
Boston Public Library, 13
Brahmins, 50-52, 67
  71-72, 88, 118, 126-127
Brooks, Charles, 171
Brotherhoods, 66
Buddha (Siddhartha
  Gautama), 17-18, 53
Buddhism, 17-20, 28-30, 53
Byzantine Empire, 8-9

Caesar, Augustus, 48
Caesar, Julius, 8, 124
Caligula, 48
Caliph, 73
Callimachus, 8
Calvin, John, 82
Calvinism, 82, 141, 147-148
Canada, 157
Capuchins, 30
Cardinals, 88
Carnegie, Andrew, 13

Castiglione,
  Baldassare, 161
Catechism, 63
Catholic priests, 75-81
Chantry schools, 109, 134
Chaplains, 90
Charlemagne, 76, 130
China:
  libraries, 8
  monks, 28
  priests, 54, 68-69
  scholars, 98-99
  schools, 166-168
  teachers, 117-118, 127-128
Chou En-lai, 167
Christian Church:
  early, 61-66
  in Middle Ages, 75-81
  *See also* Roman
  Catholic Church
Cicero, 142
Ciceronianism, 142
Circle schools, 128
Cistercians, 26, 30
Citharists, 120-121
Civil War, U.S., 12, 174
Cluny, Order of, 25
College, 169
Colonial America, 12
  teachers, 153-157
Comenius, Johann, 160
Confucianism, 54
Confucius, 98, 117-118
Conservators, 6
Constantine the Great, 125
Conventuals, 30
*Courtier, The*
  (Castiglione), 161

Courtiers, 161-162
Cubberley, Ellwood, P., 111
Cult leaders, 87
Cults, modern, 86-87
Cultural Revolution,
  Chinese, 107
Curators, 1-6
Curie, Marie, 163

Dalai Lama, 30, 31
Dame schools, 149, 173
Deaconesses, 89-90
Deacons, 64, 89
Delphic oracle, 46
Democracy, 163
Dervishes, 27-28, 75
Dewey, John, 173, 179
Dewey, Melvil, 14
Dewey decimal system, 13-14
Discipline, 159
Dissenters' Acadamies,
  153, 161
Diviners, 35, 43
Doctor of philosophy, 102-103
Dominican monks, 23-24
Domitian, 48
Druids, 72
Dueling, 162
Dziatzko, Karl, 14

Eastern Roman Empire, 66
Ebert, Fritz, 10, 13
Echkart, Meister, 23
Ecumenical movement, 91-92
Egypt:
  priests, 35-45
  scholars, 95-96
  teachers, 116-117
Elyot, Sir Thomas, 161
England, 148-153
English schoolmasters, 149-152
Erasmus Desiderius, 80, 101
Eratosthenes, 8
Europe:
  libraries, 10-12
  teachers, 129-139
Evangelists, 64
Exorcists, 35

Faith healers, 87
France, 164, 169-170
Franciscans, 25, 30

Francis of Assisi,
  Saint, 25
Franklin, Benjamin, 155
Frederick the Great, 165
Freud, Sigmund, 176
Friars, 23
Friars Minor, 30

Galileo, 104-105
Gautama. See Buddha
Germany:
  libraries, 10-11, 14
  teachers, 139-146
Gilman, Daniel Coit, 184
Goethe, Johann Wolfgang
  von, 11
Gottingen, University of, 14
Governesses, 162-163
Grammaticus, 123-125
Grammatists, 120-121
"Great Chain of Being",
  78, 84
Greece:
  priests, 45-46
  scholars, 95
  teachers, 118-123
Guidance counselors, 184
Guild schools, 134
Gurus, 29, 71

Hadith, 73
Halle, University of, 14
Haruspices, 48
Harvard University, 12
Hawley, Gideon, 110
Headmasters, 109
Henry VIII, King of
  England, 148-149
Herbart, Johann
  Friedrich, 111, 171
Herbartian movement, 171
Hermitage, Leningrad, 3
Hermits, 21
Hinduism, 49-52, 67
Historians, 96
Hitler, Adolf, 178
Humanists, 101, 136-139
Hypatia, 97

Ignatius (of) Loyola,
  Saint, 25
Imam, 74
Imbe, 70

Indenture, 131
India:
  priests, 49-53
  schools, 166
  teachers, 118, 126-127
Indiana University, 12
Indulgences, 79
Industrial Revolution,
  85, 102, 163-166
Inquisitors, papal, 23-24
Iran, 54-55
Islam:
  monks and nuns, 26-28
  priests, 72-75
  scholars, 97-98
  teachers, 128-129

Jainism, 53
Japan:
  monks, 28-29
  priests, 69-70
Jesuit Humanistic
  schools, 109
Jesuits, 25, 146, 160
Jesus, 61-62
Jewett, Charles, 13
Jews, 55-61
Jodo-Shin monks, 28
Josephus, 55-56
Judaism, 55-61
Julian the Apostate, 126
Justinian I, 126

Kannushi, 70
Karma, Law of, 52
Khatib, 74-75
Kirkpatrick, William, 179
Knights, 131
Kshatriyas, 50
Kublai Khan, 70

Lamas, 29, 90
Lancaster, Joseph, 171
La Salle, Saint Jean
  Baptiste de, 146-147
Latin, 129, 142, 151, 159
Latin America, 156-157
Legalist School, 98
Legates, 88
Leibniz, Gottfried
  Wilhelm, 10
Librarians, 7-15
Librarius, 9

Litterators, 123-124
London University
  School for
  Librarianship, 14
Loyola. *See* Ignatius
*Ludi*, 123
Luther, Martin, 83, 144-146
Lutherans, 141
*Lycee*, 169
*Lyceum*, 97

Magi, 54-55
Magicians, 34
Mahayana monks, 20
Mandala, 71
Mann, Horace, 110, 173, 174
Mantras, 71
Mary the Jewess, 97
Massachusetts Bay
  Colony, 153-154
Mass-appeal scholars, 103-104
Master craftsman, 131
Masters, 137-138
Mesopotamia:
  priests, 40-45
  teachers, 116-117
Middle Ages:
  Buddhism, 28-30
  monks and nuns, 21-26
  priests, 75-81
  teachers, 129-135
Middle class, 140-141
Military chaplains, 90
Minority groups, 177
Missionaries, 90
Missionary schools, 167
Mohammed, 73
Mohl, Robert von, 10-11
Monasteries, 66
Monitorial method, 171
Monks, 126
  Buddhist, 17-20
  Islam, 26-28
  medieval Buddhism, 28-30
  in Middle Ages, 21-26
  in modern era, 30-32
Monotheism, 55
Monsignor, 89
Mortuary priests, 37-39
*Mudras*, 71
*Muezzins*, 73-74
Museologists, 5
*Museum News*, 5

Museums, 1-5
Music teachers, 183
Mystery cults, 46

*Nakatomi*, 70
Napoleon Bonaparte, 169
Nationalism, 163
National Vocational
  Guidance Association, 184
Natural sciences, 102
Naude, Gabriel, 11
Nazi Germany, 178
Necromancy, 38
Nestorian Christians,
  8, 97, 126
New American Museum,
  N.Y., 4
New England, 153
Nichiren monks, 29, 31
Nuns:
  Buddhist, 17-18
  Islam, 26-28
  in Middle Ages, 21-26
  in modern era, 30-32

Old Testament, 55
Oswego movement, 171
Oxford University, 11-12

*Paedotribes*, 120-121
Palace Museum, Peking, 3
Palace tutors, 139
Paris, University of, 133
Parish priests, 80-81
Parish schools, 134
Parsis, 86-87
Pastors, 89
Paul, Saint, 64
Peale, Charles Willson, 4
Pedagogues, 121, 123, 184
Pergamum, Asia Minor, 7
Pestalozzi, Johann,
  111, 160, 169
Peter, Saint, 65
Petrarch, 138
Pharisees, 60-61
Philosophers, 96
Physical education, 183
Plato, 95, 97
Polytheism, 35
Pope, 78, 88
Prayer wheels, 71
Preachers, 64

*Precentor*, 9
Preparators, 6
Presbyters, 64
Priests, 34-35, 126
  Druids, 72
  in early
    Christianity, 61-66
  in Eastern and
    Central Asia,
    54-55, 67-72
  in Greece and Rome, 45-49
  in India, 49-53
  Islam, 72-75
  Jewish, 55-61
  in Middle Ages, 75-81
  modern cults, 86-87
  in Near East, 35-45
  occupations of, 87-92
  in Protestant
    Reformation, 81-86
Primary normal schools, 169-173
Principals, 110
Printing press, 140
Private schools,
  colonial, 155
Progressive movement, 179-180
Prophets, 56-58
Proselytes, 64
Protestantism, 81-86
Protestant ministers, 81-86
Protestant Reformation,
  30, 109
  priests, 81-86
  scholars, 101
  teachers, 139-146
Protestant work ethic, 141
Prussia:
  school
    administrators, 111
  teachers, 161,
    164-166, 169
Public libraries, 13
Public Libraries Act, 13
Public schools,
  colonial, 155
Public schools,
  England, 149
Punishment, 159
Puritans, 82, 148, 153

Rabbis, 60
*Ratio Studorium*, 146
Realist School, 164

Rectors, 89
Reference librarians, 15
Registrars, 6
Renaissance:
  museums, 2
  teachers, 135-139
Restorers, 6
Revolutionary War, 155-156
Rhetoricians, 124-125
Roman Catholic Church, 65-66
  decline during
      Reformation, 140-143
  priests, 76-79, 88, 92
  scholars, 99-101
  teachers, 129-139
  *See also* Christianity
Roman Empire:
  and Christianity, 65-66
  libraries, 7-8
  priests, 47-49
  scholars, 96-97
  teachers, 122-126

Sadduccees, 61
*Sadhu*, 90
Sadler, Sir Michael, 112
*Samanas*, 53
*Sangha*, 17-19
*Sarume*, 70
Scholars, 94-107
Scholasticism, 84
Scholasticus, 132
School administrators, 108-113
School boards, 110
Scribes, 1-2, 36, 116
*Scriptorium*, 9
Scudder, John, 4
Scudder, John Jr., 4
Secular clergy, 148
Secular education, 165
*Servitors*, 60
Shamans, 54
Shiites, 73
Shingon monks, 29
Shinto priests, 69-70
*Sibylline Books*, 47
Simeon the Stylite, 21
Simoniac priests, 79

Sisterhoods, 66
Slaves, 121-123
Social sciences, 102
Socrates, 95, 96, 104, 119-120
*Sopherim*, 60
Sophists, 119-120
Soviet Union, 178
Spain, 9
Strayer, George D., 111
*Studium generale*, 100
Sturm, John, 160
Submasters, 138
Sufis, 26-27, 75
Sunnis, 73
Swami, 90
Synagogue, 59

T'ang dynasty, 127-128
Tantrism, 71
Taoism, 68-69
Teachers, 115
  in Colonial America, 153-157
  in early modern
      times, 146-148
  in East, 117-118,
      126-129, 166-168
  in England, 148-153
  in Greece, 118-122
  in Industrial
      Revolution, 163-166
  in Middle Ages, 129-135
  modern era, 176-185
  in Near East, 116-117
  professionalism of, 168-176
  in Protestant
      Reformation, 139-146
  in Renaissance, 135-139
  in Roman Empire, 122-126
  transition period
      for, 157-163
Teachers' College,
  Columbia Univ., 173, 179
Teachers' unions, 181
Teacher-training
  institutes, 160
Temple at Jerusalem, 58-60
Temple prostitutes, 42
Tendai monks, 29

Therapeutae order, 21
Theravadin monks, 19-20
Tibet, 29-30, 31, 70-71
Tibetan monks, 29-30
Torah, 60
*Training of the
  Librarian, The*
  (Ebert), 10
Trappists, 30
Trustees, 109
Tutankhamen, King of
  Egypt, 44
Tutors, private, 162

Udall, Nicholas, 151
*Ulama*, 73-74
United States:
  libraries, 12-13
  museums, 4
  school
      administrators, 111-113
  schools, 164, 170-176
University, 99-100
University professors, 133
Upanishads, 53
*Urabe*, 70

*Vedas*, 49, 51, 118
Vernacular schools,
  138-139, 141-142
Vicars, 88
Vocational counselors, 184
Vocational education,
  130-131, 183

Winsor, Justin, 13
Women, 79, 86, 97, 106,
  173-176, 181
Wu, 54

Yale University, 103
Yates, Andrew J., 172

Zen monks, 28-29
Zenodotus, 8
Zoroaster, 55
Zoroastrianism, 55